Palisades.
Pure Romance.

FICTION THAT FEATURES CREDIBLE CHARACTERS AND

ENTERTAINING PLOT LINES, WHILE CONTINUING TO UPHOLD

STRONG CHRISTIAN VALUES. FROM HIGH ADVENTURE

TO TENDER STORIES OF THE HEART, EACH PALISADES

ROMANCE IS AN UNDILUTED STORY OF LOVE,

FROM BEGINNING TO END!

A PALISADES CONTEMPORARY ROMANCE

ANGEL VALLEY

PEGGY DARTY

PALISADES

ANGEL VALLEY
published by Palisades
a part of the Questar publishing family

© 1995 by Peggy Darty
International Standard Book Number: 0-88070-778-X

Cover illustration by George Angelini
Cover designed by David Carlson and Mona Weir-Daly
Edited by Deena Davis

Printed in the United States of America

For information:
QUESTAR PUBLISHERS, INC.
POST OFFICE BOX 1720
SISTERS, OREGON 97759

For all of my wonderful family:
Landon, Steve and Darla
Lan, Susan and David
and
especially my mother, Ruth Watts.

In everything, do to others what you would have
them do to you...

MATTHEW 7:12

One

L aurel Hollingsworth, don't say I didn't warn you!"

Ted Fisher, principal of Angel Valley Junior High, looked across his desk at the slim blonde woman. Shoulder-length hair styled in a smooth cut framed her oval face and delicate features.

"All right, you've warned me, Ted. But we're only talking about a summer job. Besides, I dealt with difficult children in Atlanta during my first year of teaching." Laurel smiled at the small graying man, thinking how protective he was of his teachers and students.

"And you couldn't wait to get back to the Smoky Mountains!" he teased.

"You're right! And lucky for me, your seventh-grade teacher had decided to retire."

"Lucky for us, you mean! You're one of the best teachers we've ever had. That's why you won Teacher of the Year."

"I bribed the judges," she quipped.

"Nonsense. You have a special way with children." Ted was

well aware of how Laurel threw herself into her work, giving every ounce of energy and knowledge to the students she taught. "Have I ever told you what Matilda Bennett, whom we all know is critical, said about you?"

Laurel lifted an eyebrow. "Maybe you'd better keep it to yourself."

"She said, 'Laurel Hollingsworth can light up a room with her sparkling eyes and warm smile.' She also said you're the darling of Angel Valley."

Laurel stared at Ted, then shook her head. "That's very sweet, but Mrs. Bennett wasn't around when I spoke my mind at the teachers' meeting."

"You were simply refusing to compromise your convictions. There's nothing wrong with that."

"Ted," she said gently, "you seem to be tiptoeing around something. What is it?"

"I'm wondering if I should be recommending you to this haughty-sounding socialite from Atlanta and her emotionally troubled daughter. When she called to inquire about a tutor, she told me that her daughter, Anna Lee, had gone into a depression after her father's death. Now she's fallen behind in her studies and needs to be brought up to eighth-grade level before the next school term. I know you could do it, but do you want to spend your summer that way?"

Laurel nodded thoughtfully. "Are the Wentworths the people who built that mansion out on Raven Ridge?"

Ted grinned. "Their summer place! Incidentally, I met Anna Lee's older brother in the mayor's office when I went to discuss this year's Christmas in the Park. He seems like a nice guy."

"What was he doing in the mayor's office?" Laurel was curious.

"Asking questions about the area. He owns an investment firm in Atlanta. Maybe he's planning to put a business up here."

"I hope not! The last thing we need is an Atlanta businessman trying to change our little community when we're happy just the way we are."

Ted wasn't listening. "If he has money to invest, I should solicit for our Christmas in the Park."

"Good idea. Oh! What time is my appointment?"

Ted glanced at his watch. "Ten o'clock, and I mustn't detain you. Laurel, please don't feel compelled to take this job if you don't want it."

"Thanks, Ted. I'll let you know." Laurel stood and smiled again. Then she headed out the side door of the brick school building. She already knew what her decision would be. Until hearing about this job, the summer had stretched uneventfully before her. She had no plans for a vacation this year; she was saving every dollar for a trip to Europe next summer. She couldn't wait to tour England and France, collecting little treasures from the people and their way of life. She already had plans to display those treasures on a shelf in her classroom and use them as occasional teaching tools.

Crossing the parking lot, she glanced at the sky. Sun rays were being swallowed by gray clouds. She hoped that wasn't a bad omen about her interview with the Wentworths.

Laurel's mind raced on to Anna Lee Wentworth as she hopped into her red compact car and cranked the engine. Laurel understood the pain of losing a father at an early age. It had happened to her. She had been devastated by grief until her Sunday school teacher had given her some special Bible verses. She had memorized those verses, reciting them to herself whenever the dark moments came. And slowly she began to heal.

Laurel drove from the parking lot onto the main street of Angel Valley, Tennessee and glanced up at the Smoky Mountains layered against the horizon. Early morning mist shrouded the peaks in a blue haze, reminding Laurel of the Cherokee words for their mountains: place of blue smoke. All of her life she had loved them, gaining strength and peace simply by gazing at them.

Main Street stretched lazily before her, a neat arrangement of frame and concrete buildings that defied time and weather. Folks breathed a sigh of relief when a four-lane highway was put through over in Newton, steering traffic away from Angel Valley. While neighboring towns like Gatlinburg and Pigeon Forge were bursting with progress, Angel Valley fought against change, holding tight to history and tradition. Several small businesses served the community well—a hardware store, dress shop, post office, drug store, two service stations, and two groceries. The school sat on one end of town, the church and cemetery on the other.

Laurel decided to make a quick stop at the post office to check her mail, hoping for a letter from her mother and Hal. She wheeled into a parking space beside the post office and cut her engine. As she hopped out, a gleaming black Jeep parked two spaces down caught her eye. Someday she hoped to have a vehicle like that one, which was far more suitable for traveling up to Knoxville or over to Asheville during the winter months.

She glanced at her watch, suddenly aware she was going to be late for her appointment if she didn't hurry. Her steps quickened on the pavement as she pushed through the front door with a force that sent her smack into the broad chest of a tall man dressed in Levis and a red polo.

"Ooops, sorry." The deep voice above her belonged to a very

handsome man; in fact, Laurel found herself temporarily tongue-tied as she looked up at him, the definition of tall, dark, and handsome. He was over six feet tall, with long legs and broad shoulders. Thick, dark hair framed a square face with nice features, deep blue eyes, and a smile that had paralyzed her.

"Excuse me." His smile widened as he gently sidestepped her and pushed through the door.

Laurel took a deep breath and turned to the postmistress. "Millie, who was that?"

The thin, gray-haired woman peered at Laurel over her glasses as she sorted through a stack of mail. "Don't know. He just breezed in and dropped a letter in the slot. Want me to check it out?"

"No, I'm in a hurry. Just keep an eye out." *As though she wouldn't!* Laurel thought. "Did I get a letter from Mom?"

"Laurel, you know this is the first real vacation they've had! Since they're spending the summer in New England, you can't expect Thelma to write every day."

"Mil-lie!"

"Nothing since the postcard from Boston."

Millie felt it was her duty to be mother hen to everyone in Angel Valley. This included reading over the postcards she sorted. She was, however, a kind and generous woman, the first to arrive on the doorstep with food whenever there was an illness or death. And her peanut brittle was legendary.

Laurel waved to Millie and dashed out the door, searching for the handsome stranger. He was nowhere in sight. Just her luck. She did notice, as she jumped back in her car, that the Jeep was gone. The man and his Jeep were definitely worth pursuing! A romantic notion stirred for the first time since Ryan Thompson had put a bruise on her heart.

She backed out into the street and headed toward Raven Ridge. A light mist was starting to fall, prompting Laurel to turn on her windshield wipers. Fumbling through her purse, she retrieved the eyeglasses prescribed for driving. Hating the feel of frames on her face, she abandoned glasses most of the time, but today, wanting to do all the right things, she clamped them on. As the turnoff to Raven Ridge loomed ahead, she applied the brake, slowing to make a left turn.

The road snaked up the side of the mountain, and her little car sputtered a protest as she pressed the accelerator.

"Behave," she scolded, peering right to left, eager to see the house that had caused so much speculation.

Several impressive homes had been built in the area after outsiders discovered its cool air and tranquil lifestyle, but the Wentworth mansion was reported to outdo all of them.

Although she was almost five feet six inches, Laurel kept stretching her neck to see over the hood of her car. The road was steep and narrow, switching right to left, climbing past a woods of tall pines. She topped the last hill and there it was: a magnificent, two-story, stone-and-glass structure that seemed to perch on the very top of the world.

Parking beside a black Mercedes, she reached for her purse. She had never been shy, but Ted's warning and the imposing mansion had brought on the same apprehension as a trip to the dentist.

The job will last only a couple of months, she reminded herself, thinking of the money she could tuck away in her savings. Visions of Big Ben and the Eiffel Tower danced in her head, and she took a deep breath and peered into the back seat for her umbrella. Naturally, this was the day she had left it at home.

Sighing, she hopped out of the car and gave the door a push. It's sharp corner caught her leg and she winced and bit her lip. She wasn't hurt, but now a one-inch run in her hose zipped from her ankle to her knee. *What else could go wrong?* she wondered as she made a dash up the stone walkway to the shelter of a small porch.

Her eyes flew over her navy dress, grateful she was not drenched, as she lifted the brass knocker then jumped when it made a loud BANG.

Tucking her purse under her arm, she surveyed the landscape while waiting for someone to answer the door. The valley—complete with a church steeple and farm houses—resembled Rockwell miniatures at Christmas time.

The door swung open and Laurel faced a tall, thin woman wearing a gray linen pants suit. The woman looked to be in her upper forties or early fifties, judging from the wrinkles bracketing her eyes and mouth. Her brown hair was worn short and straight, whisked back on the sides of her thin face. The russet blush on her sunken cheeks had been applied with a heavy hand, along with the brick-colored lipstick, which merely accented the thinness of her lips. Her eyes were a cold, biting blue.

"Good morning, I'm Laurel Hollingsworth. I'm here to speak with Mrs. Wentworth about a—"

"Come in!"

The woman's abrasive manner shocked Laurel as she crossed the threshold into a slate-tiled foyer.

"This way," the woman called over her shoulder, as she set off down the hall.

Glancing at oil paintings on the walls, Laurel hurried to keep up, following the woman into a huge room where crystal-globed lights danced and twinkled. It was the most gorgeous room Laurel had ever seen.

The house had been created as an extension of the mountains, with entire walls of tinted glass. Between the glass walls, cream-colored panels reached to cathedral ceilings supported by massive beams. At the far end, a huge fireplace held copper and brass. Beside it sat a large, well-stocked woodbox. A sprawling, over-stuffed sofa was flanked by chairs and ottomans upholstered in the same cream, coral, and green as the sofa.

Lush plants filled every corner, along with potted trees, and there were several crystal vases filled with fresh flowers. Richly colored Oriental rugs added warmth to the hardwood floor gleaming at Laurel's feet.

"I'm Madeline Wentworth," the woman said abruptly, turning to Laurel and motioning her to a chair.

"It's nice to meet you," Laurel said, taking a seat.

"Did you bring a résumé?" Madeline asked. Her pale blue eyes swept Laurel up and down.

Laurel bit her lip, wondering why she had overlooked something so important.

"No, I didn't. Mr. Fisher contacted me as I was about to leave town and I came right over."

Madeline looked thoughtful as she lit a cigarette. Laurel watched the woman's jaws sink into deep hollows as she inhaled the smoke.

Laurel cleared her throat, trying not to cough. "I graduated from Lee College with honors," Laurel said. "Then I taught a year in Marietta. The principal's name—"

"Never mind," Madeline waved a jeweled hand. "If you are as capable as your principal says, I don't need a résumé. The important thing is for you to help Anna Lee."

"Well, I believe—"

"Talking about me again, Mother?" A thin insolent voice spoke up.

Laurel turned in her seat and glanced over her shoulder.

Anna Lee Wentworth was short, and Laurel judged her to be at least thirty pounds overweight. Her hair was a dull brown, styled in a short straight bob; her eyebrows were badly in need of tweezers. With all their money, Laurel wondered why the girl had never had a lesson in makeup. At least her skin was smooth, without the acne typical in many girls her age.

Laurel could see little resemblance between mother and daughter, except for the blue eyes. Mrs. Wentworth was almost anorexic, which gave her features a pinched look, while Anna Lee was round in body and face, with full lips thrust into a sullen pout.

The buttons on her embroidered denim shirt were about to pop from the strain of holding cloth together, while the designer jeans were at least two sizes too small. Laurel felt sad just looking at the girl, who had a habit of tugging the front of her shirt lower over her waistline, which Laurel suspected was unbuttoned to accommodate her bulging weight.

"Hello, dear." Madeline got up from the sofa and crossed the room to her daughter's side. "Come meet your new tutor." She placed a hand on her daughter's shoulder.

Anna Lee shrugged her mother's hand away with a disgusted sigh and sauntered into the room.

Laurel stood. "Hi. My name is Laurel Hollingsworth."

19

Anna Lee glared at her, making no response.

"Anna Lee!" her mother prompted under her breath.

Anna Lee's gaze crawled down Laurel's navy dress and widened on her right leg. Then a smirk curled her lips. Laurel glanced down at the run in her hose, then back at Anna Lee and Madeline, who was now staring at the run, too.

"I don't normally run around with torn hose," Laurel said lightly, trying to make a joke of the incident. "The car door caught me as I was getting out."

Madeline and Anna Lee merely stared at her, not amused. Laurel took a deep breath and mentally counted to ten. *So much for this interview,* she decided, preparing to leave, when Anna Lee suddenly made an outburst, startling her mother as well as Laurel.

"I don't want a tutor!" She glared at her mother. "I told you before we left Atlanta, I can't concentrate. It's no use!"

Laurel heard the desperation in Anna Lee's voice and suddenly saw her as a frustrated girl hiding behind a façade of anger. Laurel's mind slipped back over the years to that miserable time in her life when she had lost her father at fourteen. She, too, had been overcome with emotions that were difficult to handle. Remembering that trying period, her heart softened as she looked at this pitiful girl who seemed to be trapped in a world of anger and bitterness.

I'll try one more time, Laurel decided.

"I think it would be easier for you to concentrate if you enjoyed your studies. I take field trips with my students and we do lots of projects that really are fun."

Anna Lee and Madeline stared at Laurel as though she were speaking in a foreign language.

"We would take a field trip along the parkway to study the different plants and flowers, and compare them to those in your science book. As for history, I ordered some special books that my students thought were pretty neat."

Laurel read the doubt on Anna Lee's face. Yet, for the first time, there was a different look in her eyes. Laurel hesitated for a moment, glancing from Anna Lee to Madeline Wentworth. "At this time of year it would be a shame not to make the most of being outdoors. I think we could do some hiking, as well."

A spark lit Madeline's dull blue eyes. "A hike? Anna Lee never exercises, so a hike sounds good, don't you think?" She turned to her sulking daughter.

"I don't feel like hiking," Anna Lee snapped.

Laurel took a deep breath. "Well, it's up to you. Perhaps you might want to try another tutor, Mrs. Wentworth." She reached for her purse.

"Okay!" Anna Lee cried. "You can be my tutor. I don't care!"

Heavy steps resounded over the hardwood floor as Anna Lee charged from the room, moving with a speed that surprised Laurel.

Madeline Wentworth stared after the girl, then reached for another cigarette. Her thin face registered weariness and defeat.

"Anna Lee sank into a deep depression after Wilson's death," Madeline said. "She's had a terrible time."

As Laurel looked at the woman's thin face and sunken eyes, it was obvious Madeline had suffered, too.

"Do you want the job?" she asked solemnly.

Laurel considered her options. She faced a tremendous challenge at a time meant for rest and relaxation after a busy school year. With Anna Lee's steps thudding in her ears, Laurel glanced down the hall, wondering why she continued to feel pulled toward this girl. Was she a glutton for punishment?

Suddenly she knew why. Embedded in her mind was the hand-lettered verse, made and framed by a student, resting on her desk at school. The sign seemed to flash before her eyes: *Do unto others as you would have them do unto you.*

Laurel thought of the kind, caring teacher who had gone out of her way to help when Laurel's father died. Now she had been offered a chance to do for someone else what had once been done for her. Long ago Laurel had made a commitment to help troubled children. Here was the perfect opportunity.

She took a deep breath. "Yes, I do."

"Good," Madeline sighed. She walked over to a desk, opened the drawer, and removed a checkbook. "Did Mr. Fisher mention the salary?"

"Yes, he did."

The salary was great, but that was no longer her reason for taking the job. When she saw Madeline reaching for a pen, Laurel spoke up. "Mrs. Wentworth, why don't you wait until I've worked a week before you pay me?"

Madeline eyed her sharply. "I hope that doesn't mean you'll up and quit if you don't like the job. I can't go looking for another tutor; there isn't time."

"If I take the job, I'll keep it," Laurel answered smoothly, trying to ignore Madeline's sharp tone. "I'm just not comfortable with being paid in advance."

Madeline's thin brows arched. "You will be able to begin tomorrow, won't you?" she inquired.

Do I have a choice? Laurel almost asked. "I suppose I can."

"Then we'll count it a full week." She was making a note on the inside of her checkbook.

"That won't be necessary," Laurel responded. "I only expect to be paid for the days I work."

Madeline stared at her, her eyes narrowing for a moment as though she were suspicious of that answer.

Laurel turned to go. "It was nice meeting you, Mrs. Wentworth."

"Thank you." Despite a brief smile, Madeline's voice was still cold and uncaring.

As Laurel left the house, she was relieved to see the rain had stopped. She got in the car and cranked the engine, glancing again at the house. As her eyes moved up to the second level, she saw Anna Lee standing before a window, staring down at her.

Laurel waved, but Anna Lee merely turned away. Heaving a frustrated sigh, Laurel drove carefully down the winding drive. *This could be the most difficult job I've ever taken,* she decided, as she turned back onto the highway. Still, she felt led to do it. Engrossed in thought as she drove along, she almost missed the black Jeep.

He swept by without looking in her direction, but Laurel caught a glimpse of the handsome stranger she had seen in the post office, the owner of the Jeep. Her eyes shot to her rearview mirror, hurriedly reading the license plate as his turn signal began to flash. Georgia. The Jeep shot from the highway up the road to Raven Ridge.

Who is he? she wondered. *And what business does he have with the Wentworths?*

Two

L aurel had always drawn strength from her Granny Hollingsworth, who was as refreshing as an evening rain after a blistering summer day. After meeting the Wentworths, Laurel felt a longing to see the one woman who could restore her good spirits. And that, of course, was Granny.

Betsy Hollingsworth was an original mountain woman with a head full of common sense. Thinking of Granny, Laurel smiled to herself as she headed to her grandmother's farm on the edge of town. Along the way she waved to Mable Harper, out checking the effects of the rain on her vegetable garden, then to Florence Stockton, inspecting her tomatoes.

The people in Angel Valley lived close to the earth. They planted and harvested their vegetables and flowers, allowing for the occasional bad seed that would sprout and run wild. Like human beings, Granny said. When a vegetable crop or flower garden failed, folks simply planted again and hoped for the best. There was respect and tolerance for nature with its strengths and weaknesses, and for that reason, Laurel never fretted for long over rain or wind or heat. Like her ancestors, she had learned not to brood about something over which she had no control.

As she approached the land that had belonged in her family for a hundred years, she breathed a sigh of contentment. Granny's farm brought a sense of security, wrapping around her like an afghan on a frosty winter night.

Going away to college had been difficult for Laurel, but it was during those years that her mother began to see Hal Hartley, a widower. After four years, her mother finally agreed to marry Hal, and they seemed happy together.

As Laurel's car rounded the corner, Granny's frame house behind the picket fence came into view. She wheeled into the driveway, automatically tooting her horn. It was something her father had always done, letting Granny know that family, not unexpected company, was arriving. While Laurel kept up the tradition, it never seemed to matter to Granny who came, for there was always enough food on the stove and lots more in the refrigerator.

Laurel dashed across the yard to the front porch, glancing at the comfortable rockers and the colorful geraniums growing profusely in their clay pots. She opened the screen, tapped lightly on the door, then turned the knob. Unlocked, as usual.

"It's me," Laurel called.

"I'm in the kitchen," the familiar voice answered.

She glanced around, absorbing the familiar surroundings. Her eyes swept the pine paneling on the long room that served as a living-dining room. Granny's white doilies were scattered about the tables and chairs, along with her knitted afghans, which covered the lumps in the Duncan Phyfe sofa.

Laurel paused at the dining room table where squares of printed fabric were neatly arranged. Granny had the instincts of an artist in creating a design. She could take a batch of scraps and, with the right arrangement of color and shading, produce something lovely.

"Are you starting another quilt?" Laurel called, hesitating at the table to touch a soft floral square.

"Sadie Birdsong is in a bad way."

"So you're making her a quilt?" Laurel stepped to the kitchen door.

"A quilt is like a hug," Granny glanced over her shoulder.

Granny was a small woman, scarcely over five feet tall and weighing only one hundred pounds, yet she had given birth to three strong sons and had been a good wife to her husband of thirty years until his death. She wore Reeboks, faded jeans, and cotton shirts most of the time, the exception being Sunday morning when she donned a dress for Sunday school and church. She stood at the kitchen cabinet, inspecting a green tomato.

"What're you making?" Laurel asked, giving her grandmother a hug.

Canning jars lined the counter beside a huge pan of green tomatoes, a bottle of vinegar, and a box of brown sugar.

"Green tomato relish. At least I hope that's what it turns out to be. Let's have some coffee."

"With a serving of green tomato relish?" Laurel grinned.

"How about pound cake?"

"I don't need the pound! But I'm not hungry, thanks. Just coffee will be fine."

Laurel's eyes were filled with love as she watched her grandmother dash a hand over the short brown hair, streaked with gray above the ears. She darted around the kitchen, scooping sugar from the canister, retrieving the pitcher of cream from the refrigerator.

Granny's keen brown eyes swept Laurel as she motioned her to the round oak table. "Why are you so dressed up on a weekday?" she inquired.

"I had a meeting." Laurel glanced at the huge pot on the stove. "And why are you making so much relish?"

"To put in the booth at the fair this weekend."

"The crafts fair! I had completely forgotten."

"Well, don't forget the dunking machine."

Laurel groaned. "Wish I hadn't gotten roped into that."

"It's a good cause," Granny reminded her.

The community sponsored a fair the first week in June, with the ladies donating crafts to sell while the men served as vendors for pizza and cotton candy, and a dunking machine, all to benefit the community's needs. This year their mission was new equipment for the volunteer fire department.

"I'm glad you reminded me about the fair. Time flies," Laurel added, cupping her chin in her hands, thinking that she'd been back in Angel Valley for over a year now.

"Only when you're having fun," Granny winked. "And speaking of fun, tell me what you've been doing." She poured coffee from her aging percolator into delicate cups, then settled into her chair, her hands folded on the table.

Laurel leaned back against the yellow gingham cushions and tilted her head thoughtfully. "I have something interesting to tell you."

Granny's dark eyes twinkled in her small oval face. "You've met a man."

"Granny! Will you please stop trying to marry me off? No, I haven't met anyone who interests me…"

An image of the tall dark stranger in the post office came to mind, but she dared not mention him. Within the hour, Granny would be on the phone to Millie, conspiring with her to find out who he was and precisely what he was doing here.

"You're not trying to meet anyone," Granny protested. "Now listen to me, hon. Just because that city slicker turned out to be a rotten apple, that doesn't mean—"

"Please! Spare me the one-bad-apple-doesn't-spoil-the-crate speech." She patted Granny's hand. "Just kidding. And I'm a big girl now. I know one bad relationship shouldn't cause me to run from all men. Frankly, Ryan had more problems than just being 'a city slicker,' as you put it." She shook her head at that expression as she poured cream into her coffee and reached for the sugar. "As a matter of fact, I've met some very nice city slickers. I just haven't met anyone who interests me."

Granny grinned at Laurel. "Honey, when God puts the right man in your life, you'll know it, believe me."

"I believe you, but I'm twenty-five years old. Wait," Laurel put up her hand, "don't say it. I know. God is teaching me patience."

Granny laughed. "Seems like it. When I was your age, I'd already had my three sons. In fact, your daddy and mamma married in their teens."

"Thanks for making me feel better," Laurel scolded playfully. "And now I'm a bridesmaid in Jessica's wedding. First Rosemary, now Jessica. I really am beginning to feel like an old maid."

"Nonsense! How is Jessica, by the way? I haven't seen her in years."

"Happy, I suppose. I've only seen her a few times since her family moved away, but we still talk on the phone from time to time." Laurel stared into space. "You know she hated Louisville. That's why she's coming back here to get married."

Granny nodded and took a sip of her coffee. "What were you going to tell me?"

"Mr. Fisher recommended me for a tutoring job with an Atlanta family who is spending the summer here. The daughter's grades have slipped since the death of her father." She fell silent. There was no point in detailing the problem to Granny; she'd only worry.

"What sort of folks are they?" Granny asked interestedly.

Laurel studied the dainty blue flowers on her china cup, thinking of the mother and daughter who seemed so at odds with one another. "Their name is Wentworth and they're from Atlanta. They're the folks who built the big house on Raven Ridge."

"Oh. Those folks! I hear they're filthy rich, so watch your step, young lady."

"Why do you say that?"

Granny shrugged. "You know how Mary Lou likes to gossip."

"And just what does she say about the Wentworths?"

"That every gal in town is after that young man."

"What young man? Who are you talking about?"

"The son. According to Mary Lou, he's got it all—manners, charm, looks, intelligence." Her eyes snapped wider as though something had just occurred to her. "Laurel Hollingsworth, watch your step!"

Laurel chewed the inside of her lip, wondering if the man in the black Jeep was Anna Lee's older brother. "You needn't worry," Laurel sighed. "If he's related to the two females I just met, he wouldn't appeal to me. Once I got to know him, that is." *Looks weren't everything, that was for sure!*

She finished her coffee and stood. "I'd better run. And you need to get back to your relish."

"I'm going to put a quart of relish in the food booth, and I guess I'll donate a quilt. The committee is yelling for quilts. Maybe I'll win a blue ribbon," she looked back at Laurel and winked.

"Is that the prize? A blue ribbon for a valuable quilt? How cheap!" They laughed together, for both knew the fair was a wonderful cause. "Just don't let all your quilts get away. I want one," Laurel reminded her.

"Yours are already packed away in the cedar chest."

"Bless you!"

"Have you heard from your mother?" Granny followed Laurel into the living room.

At the mention of her mother, Laurel wandered to the mantle, looking at the family photographs.

"One postcard from Boston. If another one comes, I'm sure Millie will recite every word to you." Laurel lifted the antique frame that held the wedding picture of her mother and father.

"Your mother was a good wife to my son," Granny said, looking at the picture. "I love her like a daughter, and I want to see her happy. I like Hal," she added.

Laurel studied the photograph. Her mother wore a white satin wedding dress with lace sleeves and collar. Her blonde head was tilted back as she looked adoringly at Jim Hollingsworth. He was tall, with brown hair and eyes, large features, and a smile that stretched from ear to ear.

Granny's hand clamped Laurel's shoulder. "He would have been so proud of you."

Laurel drew a deep breath and turned back to her grandmother. "I was always proud of him."

Granny nodded. "Your father did a lot to help folks enjoy the park with those hiking and horseback trails and fire control roads he helped build." She slipped her hand around Laurel's arm as they walked to the front door. "And now I can see that you carry on his dream of conservation, in your own way, of course."

As they reached the front door, Granny looked out across the level green meadow that stretched to the highway. "I wish my other sons had stayed here, but they wanted to go out and see the world, and I couldn't hold them back."

Laurel's father had been the oldest of Granny's three sons; the middle son, Frank, was a furniture salesman in Raleigh, and the youngest, Bill, made a military career for himself.

Laurel looked down at her petite grandmother. *She must get lonely,* Laurel thought, *yet she never complains.*

"Granny, how about an afternoon of bargain-hunting in Asheville? Want to?"

"You know me better than that. I do my shopping here or from the catalog. I'm not one for fashion. Anyway, my daughters-in-law keep me in fashion with their gifts at birthdays and Christmas."

"Okay," Laurel replied, giving Granny a hug.

She hurried out the door, wondering why her grandmother

was so different from most women when it came to shopping. She'd much rather putter around her yard or her kitchen, or make quilts. She spent her winter evenings knitting sweaters for family and friends or anyone in the community who needed a good, warm sweater. And even though she'd had her share of struggles, Granny was one of the happiest people Laurel had ever known.

As Laurel slid into the leather seat of her car and started the engine, her mind began to spin with ideas for tutoring Anna Lee. She drove toward the school, wanting to chat with Ted Fisher and search around for the best resource materials.

When she arrived at the Wentworth house the next morning, a pleasant, dark-haired woman answered the door. The woman wore a white blouse and a denim skirt and greeted Laurel as though she knew her.

"Good morning, I'm Laurel Hollingsworth. I'll be Anna Lee's tutor for the summer."

"I'm Lou," the woman replied, though her smile began to fade. "I'm afraid Mrs. Wentworth and her daughter are still asleep."

"Oh." Laurel glanced at her watch. "I assumed I was to come at eight. I guess I should have asked."

"Miss Hollingsworth—"

"Please call me Laurel."

"Laurel, why don't you come on in and have a cup of tea?"

Laurel hesitated, wondering what to do. "I suppose there's no point in driving back to town."

"No. Please come in."

Laurel took a firmer grip on her briefcase, loaded with books and notes, as she followed Lou into the room that had impressed her so. She parked her briefcase on the coffee table and took a seat by the window. As she looked over the room, admiring its beauty, she heard the sound of a vehicle coming up the drive. She glanced over her shoulder out a window that overlooked a corner of the yard and the woods to the side of the house; the driveway was blocked from view.

At that moment, Lou entered the room carrying a tray with silver service. Laurel wondered if Mrs. Wentworth kept an extra set of silver and fine china here at her summer house. Again, the wealth of the Wentworth family amazed her.

"You taught my grandson last year," Lou said, as she placed the tray on the coffee table and poured Laurel a cup of tea.

"I did?" Laurel studied the woman, whose black hair was wound into shiny braids on the top of her head.

"John Whiteside," Lou supplied proudly.

"John! He was one of my brightest students. I adored him." She remembered well the shy Cherokee boy with the sharp mind.

"And you're his favorite teacher."

"Thanks. How is he doing?"

"Very well."

Laurel reached for her tea. "Will you please say hello for me when you see him?"

"Of course."

As Lou left the room, Laurel pondered over a trip to Lone Oak to visit the camp. She'd heard wonderful things about their work with underprivileged children. Suddenly, her thoughts were interrupted by male voices just beyond the window.

"I want to build a barbecue pit and picnic area up on that next ridge," a baritone voice announced.

"Quite a view you'd have up there," a deeper one responded.

"I believe in enjoying nature. It's a free gift; most people forget that."

Those words intrigued Laurel, for the voice spoke her own sentiments. She couldn't resist turning in her chair to peer out the window. *Who was down there?*

A middle-aged man dressed in work clothes and cowboy hat came into view and was speaking again.

"Want me to haul the lumber up there in my truck, Mr. Wentworth?"

"Yes, please."

The owner of the voice stepped into her line of vision and Laurel looked down at thick dark hair and broad shoulders stretching a white knit sports shirt. It was the man she had seen in the post office yesterday!

Mr. Wentworth! The man had called him Wentworth. She whirled around in her chair. How foolish she would feel if he turned, glanced at the window, and caught her staring or eavesdropping!

What was it Granny had said? All the women in Angel Valley were whispering about this man from Atlanta. Well, she wasn't going to get swept off her feet like she was sixteen again. He might be nice looking and come across as charming, but in his own way, he was probably as spoiled as Anna Lee.

I can handle this job, she decided, taking a sip of the smooth tea. She'd never had any trouble keeping her work and her personal life separated. She did, on occasion, worry too much about her students, even though she was constantly told to try to remain objective.

"I didn't realize you would be here so early." Madeline Wentworth stood in the door. She wore a gray satin robe with matching slippers. Obviously, she had just crawled out of bed.

Laurel glanced at her watch. It was 8:30. "I assumed you would want to keep school hours, but we can change the time to suit you."

The woman sauntered over and poured herself a cup of tea, ignoring Laurel's suggestion. Clearly, the most important thing on her mind at the moment was getting awake.

"Good grief," she snapped, after tasting the tea. "Where is that Indian woman? This is nothing more than flavored water!"

Laurel glanced down at her tea, thinking it tasted fine to her. Obviously, Mrs. Wentworth was not a morning person. Laurel decided to say nothing until the woman's mood had improved but when she charged from the room without a word, Laurel wondered exactly how long that would take.

Laurel could feel her happy mood sliding down to her toes. It was going to be a long, long summer.

Footsteps shuffled behind her. Laurel turned to face Anna Lee, tugging at her sweatshirt as she trudged into the room.

"Hi," Laurel called, placing her tea cup on the tray. "Ready to begin?"

"No. But I don't have a choice, do I?" Anna Lee glared at Laurel.

Laurel ignored the catty remark and walked over to get her briefcase.

"Where would you like to work?" Laurel asked.

Anna Lee heaved a sigh. "Mother says we can work here."

Laurel unsnapped the clasp on her briefcase and removed a large book of colorful pictures. "Look, I want to show you something."

As she spoke, she watched a tiny spark of interest flicker in Anna Lee's puffy eyes before she flopped onto the sofa. Flipping through the science book, Laurel came to a halt on a page of wildflowers.

"I'm hoping we can make that trip up the parkway in the next few days," she began cheerfully. "There are over fourteen hundred species of plants in the Smokies and—"

"Why?" Anna Lee blurted. "Why are there so many?"

Ah, a question. That's a good sign. "Rich soil and a gentle climate," Laurel answered. "Also, we can study the wildlife. Doesn't that sound like a pretty good science lab?"

Anna Lee shrugged. "Maybe."

The morning slipped by quickly, to Laurel's surprise. Although Anna Lee attempted to retain the indifference she wore like a shield, she asked an occasional question and even gave answers when called upon. But Laurel watched her carefully, secretly pleased by the expression in her eyes. The girl pondered over the pictures, studying the plants thoughtfully, finally venturing a few questions.

"Excuse me." Mrs. Wentworth stood in the door. Her short hair was combed and stiffly sprayed. She was dressed in a crisp white linen pants suit with a jeweled bodice. "Lou has our lunch if you two can break now."

"I'm starved!" Anna Lee yelled, bolting from the sofa.

Laurel followed her into a spacious dining room where

another glass wall overlooked a forest of spruce and pine. The scene provided the perfect foil for relaxing and enjoying a meal, yet neither Laurel nor Anna Lee seemed to notice.

A lace cloth covered the long dining table that held four place settings of fine china and gleaming silver. Madeline Wentworth took her seat at the head of the table and motioned Laurel to sit opposite Anna Lee. That left an empty space at the far end.

Anna Lee was already gulping her soda, while Lou painstakingly brought the platters of food out and placed them gently on the table. Sneaking a glance at Madeline, Laurel began to wonder what was troubling her. The skin around her eyes looked drawn, as though she were in pain, and her complexion had paled.

The meal consisted of fried chicken with rice and gravy and thick crusty biscuits. Laurel's eyes slipped over the food, amazed at all the calories before her. *Did Lou normally cook this way,* she wondered, *or did she prepare what Mrs. Wentworth requested?*

Laurel unfolded the white linen napkin and spread it over her lap. She wondered if she'd be able to stay awake if she ate as heartily as Anna Lee. Still, the food was delicious, and she began to enjoy her meal. When the front door banged she jumped in spite of herself.

Heavy footsteps resounded over the hardwood floors, and everyone seemed to hold their breath. Madeline looked up expectantly, and for the first time her grim expression softened in a smile.

"Dear, you're late," she said, but there was no reprimand to her tone.

"I was helping the guys with that picnic site we're building up on the ridge." The voice was directly behind Laurel. "Is there enough food for the men?"

"I instructed the cook to prepare for only four people,"

Madeline answered. "But really, Matthew, you shouldn't get so friendly with the workers. They'll be taking advantage of us, the first thing you know."

"No, they won't."

Laurel glanced up as he came into her line of vision at the end of the table. He was dressed casually in a white golf shirt and jeans. His eyes, a soft blue-gray, turned to her and Laurel felt the same jolt she had experienced yesterday.

Madeline cleared her throat. "Matthew, this is Laurel Hollingsworth. She's going to be tutoring Anna Lee this summer. Laurel, this is my son, Matthew."

"How do you do," Laurel nodded politely.

"Hello." White teeth flashed against his tanned skin. "It's a pleasure to meet you." He settled into his chair then glanced back at her. "Didn't we meet at the post office yesterday?"

"As a matter of fact, we did." She glanced at Madeline. "I was in a rush to pick up my mail and ran head-on into your son."

"I didn't mind," he said, good-naturedly, reaching for his napkin.

"Are you hungry?" Madeline asked, looking concerned. Laurel sensed that her son was just as important to this woman as her daughter. She obviously cared deeply about her children and, no doubt, wanted to be a good mother.

"I'm ravenous," Matt answered between mouthfuls, "but if I eat all this food, I may have to stretch out under a shade tree."

He grinned at Laurel, and she quickly turned her attention to her plate. Her appetite had vanished since her nerves seemed to be lodged in the pit of her stomach. She felt as though she had just stumbled into a nest of wasps and was trying to ease out before she got stung.

"I thought," he said, looking pointedly at Anna Lee, "we were going to watch our waistlines this summer."

"Not me!" Anna Lee snapped. "I'll eat whatever I want to."

"How long will it take to complete the picnic site?" Madeline intervened, glancing nervously from Anna Lee to Matt.

Laurel noticed that Madeline had placed her napkin on the table, obviously having completed her meal. The food on her plate had scarcely been touched.

"Just a few days. It's going to be great," he said, sipping his tea. "Perhaps," he glanced back at Laurel, "you and Anna Lee can do some studying up there."

"No way," Anna Lee snapped. "I'm not going way up there!"

Matt's smile disappeared as his eyes lingered on Anna Lee. Then he turned back to his food with a careless shrug. "Suit yourself."

Laurel had finished her meal, but she noticed that Anna Lee was reaching for another large chicken breast. Laurel glanced at Madeline, wondering what she thought about her daughter's voracious appetite, but she seemed oblivious to it.

"If anyone needs me this afternoon, I'll be up in my room," Madeline said in a faint voice. "I'm having one of my headaches. In fact, I think I'll go up and lie down now."

Laurel came to her feet, eager to make her own exit. The last thing she needed was to sit at the table making polite chitchat with the most attractive man she'd ever met, while his mother and sister observed with disapproving scowls.

"I enjoyed the meal," she said, focusing her attention on Madeline. "Excuse me."

Laurel hurried back to the living room. She was having enough difficulty dealing with Anna Lee and her mother; now it was quite obvious that Matthew Wentworth was going to be one more problem. A big one.

Laurel and Anna Lee worked until two in the afternoon, then Laurel decided to call it a day. After lunch, Anna Lee had been sluggish and uninterested, and Laurel found herself yawning, as well. She said goodbye to Anna Lee, hoping for a better day tomorrow.

That evening, after a leisurely bath, Laurel curled up in bed with the latest issue of her favorite magazine. She flipped through the glossy pages, hesitating on an article about the latest in fashion. After reading the same paragraph twice, however, she closed the magazine and laid it aside with a disgusted sigh. What was wrong with her? She couldn't even look at the pretty clothes without seeing the Wentworths on every page. Particularly Matt.

She turned to stare into the darkness beyond her window. What was she going to do about this silly attraction she felt for him? She had imagined that once she had a chance to observe him, she'd see that in his own way he was as spoiled as Anna Lee. On the contrary, as Ted Fisher had said, he seemed like a nice guy.

Granny was right. She'd better watch her step.

Three

The next two days passed without complications for Laurel. She asked to borrow Anna Lee's seventh-grade textbooks in order to plan her lessons. Anna Lee grudgingly obliged. After going through the books, Laurel had mapped out a plan she felt Anna Lee was ready to pursue. Slowly, Anna Lee began to show an interest in her studies. As for her attitude, when she looked at Laurel, her expression had changed from anger and resentment to mild curiosity.

To Laurel's relief, there were no more encounters with Matt Wentworth. He had returned to Atlanta to oversee an important project and was not expected back until the weekend.

When Laurel arrived on Friday morning, Madeline motioned her into the study before Anna Lee came downstairs.

"How do you think Anna Lee is doing?" Madeline asked. She was practically wringing her hands.

"I think we're making progress," Laurel replied.

Madeline sighed. "Perhaps she can go on to eighth grade without difficulty." As she spoke, her shoulders slumped forward.

Laurel thought she looked like a woman carrying a huge burden.

Suddenly Laurel was touched with concern for this woman and her problems. She gave her a warm smile. "Mrs. Wentworth, I'll do my best to see that Anna Lee enters eighth grade prepared."

"Thank you," Madeline said, attempting a smile.

Laurel went to work with renewed vigor. She took heart from her conversation with Madeline and began to feel optimistic about what she and Anna Lee could accomplish. She scheduled a meeting with the eighth-grade teacher at Angel Valley so she could refresh her memory of curriculum.

Her spirits were soaring by midmorning, but all too soon another turn of events brought complications, beginning with Matt's return from Atlanta.

Madeline, Anna Lee, and Laurel had just sat down to the table when he walked into the dining room, calling a cheerful hello.

"How was Atlanta?" Madeline asked, as he took a seat at the table and smiled around the group.

"Too hot and too populated!" He turned to Laurel. "How has your week been going, Miss Hollingsworth?"

"Fine, thank you."

He continued to stare at her for several seconds. Laurel turned her attention to her food, after glancing at Madeline and Anna Lee. Both were watching Matt curiously, and she wondered if they thought he was being too friendly with her.

"Anna Lee is making progress," Madeline spoke up.

"Good. Then why not take the afternoon off?"

All heads swiveled in his direction. "Just kidding. When I

came through town, I noticed they were putting up signs for some kind of fair this weekend. Might be fun for you ladies," he looked from Madeline to Anna Lee.

"The crafts fair is one of the highlights of the summer," Laurel spoke up, looking at Anna Lee. "You'll have to come watch me get dunked! The teachers have been recruited to sit on the dunking machine."

"Really?" Matt was fascinated. "You're going to do that?"

She nodded. "I'm hoping those who pay to throw balls at me will be poor shots." She laughed softly, unaware of the way laughter put a sparkle in her eyes.

Matt was staring at her, looking both amused and fascinated as she relayed information about the fair.

"There are games and booths and good food." She glanced at Madeline. "Proceeds from the fair go to benefit the community. My grandmother usually donates her quilts."

"Tell us about your family," Matt prompted, looking at her with interest.

Laurel wondered if he cared of if he were merely being polite. His eyes seemed to reflect a genuine interest in what she had to say as everyone sat quietly, waiting for her response.

"My parents were born and raised here," she replied. "I don't have any brothers and sisters. My father died many years ago, and my mother remarried." As she spoke, Laurel lost some of the self-consciousness that restrained her.

"I don't like this stuff!" Anna Lee burst out, tossing her fork onto the china plate with a loud clank.

Shocked, Laurel turned to stare at her. Sometimes she found it hard to believe just how badly the girl behaved.

The day's fare was a chicken salad dish with fresh fruit and Lou's homemade bread. It was the most sensible lunch that had been served since Laurel began working with Anna Lee. Laurel suspected, however, that it was not the food, but rather the topic of conversation that had upset Anna Lee. Laurel replayed her words in her mind—what had she said? *My father died…my mother remarried.…* She bit her lip, wishing she had chosen her words more carefully.

Madeline cleared her throat. "Dear, this food tastes all right, and it's very healthy." She was making a valiant effort to restore a peaceful atmosphere for those seated at the table.

"I still don't like it!" Anna Lee shouted, flinging her napkin into the middle of the table before stalking from the room.

Laurel averted her eyes, astonished all over again by Anna Lee's behavior. She suspected the girl needed therapy, and she wondered if she dared mention this to Madeline. On the other hand, Anna Lee might already be in therapy while in Atlanta.

Matt cleared his throat. "Well, Anna Lee is in her usual mood, I see."

Madeline sat pale and rigid at the end of the table. "We must be patient with her."

"You've been more than patient, Mother. I think it's time for some discipline."

Laurel lowered her eyes to her plate. She had no desire to be privy to the family's personal discussions and was wondering how she could gracefully leave the room.

"Excuse me. I'm getting a headache." Madeline pushed her chair back and came to her feet, gripping the table as though the strength had been drained from her body. "I'm going to lie down."

As she left the room, Laurel had no idea what to say or do. She searched her mind for a topic of conversation to ease the tension as she and Matt sat alone at the long table.

"You must think we're the most unstable bunch you've ever met," he said, looking at her.

Laurel swallowed, laying her knife across her plate. "No, I don't think that. I understand you've been through a tragedy, losing your father."

"You just said your father died. You seem to have survived without a chip on your shoulder, and I imagine your circumstances were not as easy as...," his voice trailed. "I'm sorry. There's no point in boring you with our problems."

"You aren't boring me," she said gently.

His eyes swept over her face, as though he wondered what she thought of them.

"Having lived away for so long, I can see the situation more objectively now. It's pretty sad," he continued.

He leaned back in the chair, hands grasped behind his head. "Dad wanted me to go to the same boys' school he had attended in Chattanooga, so I left home when I started high school." He was staring out the window. "The school was located in Dad's home town, and I spent a lot of time with his mother."

His blue eyes wandered back to Laurel and a grin softened his mouth. "Grandma is the most wonderful woman in the world."

Laurel nodded. "And Chattanooga is a nice town. I took some students there once to see Lookout Mountain, and then we went to that wonderful aquarium."

"Your students must have enjoyed that. You really try, don't you?" he asked, looking at her thoughtfully.

"I love kids and teaching, particularly here. Some of my students don't travel much. I really enjoy taking the kids to interesting places."

"That's very generous of you," he said softly. He planted his elbow on the table, cupped his chin in his hand, and stared at her.

Laurel glanced away from his direct gaze, wondering just what was going through his mind. She was glad to see Lou quietly enter the dining room to clear away the table. Lou had probably overheard the family argument and felt as awkward as Laurel. *How many other arguments had she heard?* Laurel wondered, smiling at Lou as she reached for her plate.

"Thank you," Laurel said, then looked back at Matt. "Did you attend college in Chattanooga?"

"No. After high school I entered the University of Tennessee as a business major. When I graduated, I returned to Chattanooga and went into real estate. I miss living there."

"I can understand why."

"I had to come back to Atlanta after my father died. He had built a successful investment firm that became my responsibility." He shook his head slowly. "I was hoping I could get along with Mother and Anna Lee but..."

Laurel thought she had an idea of the difficulties he must encounter with his mother and sister, not to mention the enormous challenge of running a large corporation. She hadn't imagined she would ever feel sorry for this man who seemed to have everything, but suddenly she did. The years he had spent with his grandmother had obviously been good for him, and by comparison, returning to be with Mrs. Wentworth and Anna Lee must have been difficult. Talking with him gave her a lot of insight as to the differences between him and his mother and sister. She wondered if he was like his father.

"Do you think you'll ever return to Chattanooga? Perhaps open an office there?" she asked.

"No. I'm stuck in Atlanta for now. If I had a choice, I'd live here in the Smokies. This is a great place."

"Yes, it is. I taught in Marietta for a year. Junior high."

"How did you like living there?" he asked.

"The Atlanta area is a great place to visit, but it never felt like home. I suppose no other place would interest me for long. I'm too happy here in the mountains. And fortunately," she smiled, "I wasn't one of those people who complained about being bored and wanting to leave here."

"Fortunately?"

"I didn't give folks an opportunity to say 'I told you so' when I returned. The truth is, I was always happy here, but I felt I should try another lifestyle. After listening to some of my friends in college, I began to think life in a big city was what I needed." She laughed. "Boy, was I mistaken!"

"What makes this area so special?"

"It's guarded by the angels," she answered seriously.

"You think so?" he asked with a wry grin.

She smiled. "Sometimes it seems that way. But, really, I like it here because people move at a slower pace and have the same values." She bit her lip, aware that she was getting into a subject that might prove uncomfortable for both of them. It was easy to forget who he was, as they sat at the dining table, talking casually about their lives.

"I see." His gaze slipped over her face. "Would you like to have dinner with me tonight?"

The question caught her by surprise. While it seemed to be a spur of the moment suggestion, he was looking at her as though he hoped she would say yes. It was the last thing she expected, and for a moment she was unable to think of a reply, much less verbalize it. While she would have loved to go to dinner with the charming man, she knew it was out of the question.

"I'm sorry," she looked at him and smiled. "I already have plans." *Like grading your sister's papers!*

He nodded. "I expected that."

"Thank you anyway," she said, coming to her feet. She wondered how long they had been sitting here engrossed in conversation. Madeline was sure to disapprove if she had checked on her. "Well," she glanced toward the living room, "perhaps I'll go look for Anna Lee."

He stood, looking at her with an odd expression, one she couldn't read. "I've enjoyed talking with you," he said.

She nodded, then walked out of the room, feeling happy for a change. Her conversation with Matt had done wonders for her morale. She settled down in the living room, waiting for Anna Lee to return. Fortunately, she didn't have to wait long. Only five minutes had passed when Anna Lee sidled into the room and picked up a book as though nothing had happened.

The remainder of the day passed uneventfully as Anna Lee remained subdued and unresponsive. Laurel tried to concentrate on their work, but her mind kept sneaking back to Matt. Finally, as Laurel and Anna Lee were closing the books and putting away pens and notebooks, Madeline walked into the living room.

"Here." She thrust a check at Laurel.

Laurel looked up, somewhat startled by Madeline's blunt tone of voice. "I've enjoyed working with Anna Lee," she said, glancing at her pupil who had resumed her expression of indifference. *At least, that was better than a pout,* she decided, glancing back at Madeline, whose mood seemed to have darkened.

She has a headache, Laurel reminded herself, noticing that Madeline was looking at her a bit differently. *Was it the facial expression or the look in her eyes?* Laurel wondered, then decided it was her eyes; sleepy, glazed. She had obviously taken medication for the headache.

Behind them, Anna Lee's footsteps thudded over the board floors as she left without a goodbye. Trying to retain a mood of cheerfulness, despite the gloom around her, Laurel gathered up papers and pens.

"I'll see you next week, Anna Lee," Laurel called, zipping up her briefcase.

Without a word, Madeline turned around and left the room. Laurel stared after her, releasing a deep sigh. She was glad the week was finally over, and turned her thoughts toward something fun—the crafts fair on Saturday. She was about to leave when she spotted her tea cup and decided to return it to the kitchen. Halfway down the hall, however, she overheard a conversation not meant for her ears.

"Matthew, I heard you ask that young woman out to dinner this evening." Madeline's voice came from around the corner.

Laurel stopped abruptly. She had no intention of eavesdropping; in fact, she wished she could magically disappear through the wall to the car, but there was no way to retreat gracefully without being heard.

Matt was making some response; unlike his mother, however, he had the tact to lower his voice. While the words were muffled, there was no mistaking the sharp edge to his voice.

"But you have enough girlfriends in Atlanta," Madeline snapped. "There's no need to add a little mountaineer—"

"She's an intelligent, well-educated woman." His voice was still low, but now the words were distinguishable.

"Who still has a twang to her voice. And she has no sense of fashion. She's a mountaineer! You don't need to add her to your list of conquests!"

The words were like a physical blow to Laurel, but somehow she managed to turn on her heel and head for the living room, less careful now to muffle her footsteps. She placed her cup on the coffee table and grabbed her briefcase. To her annoyance, she felt tears prick her eyes as she snatched up her purse and dashed out the front door.

Laurel told herself she shouldn't let Madeline's ugly remarks upset her, but the conversation she had overheard evoked an old memory that still rankled. As her feet flew down the stone walkway, cool air washed over her face, soothing her burning cheeks. She took a deep breath, trying to calm her nerves and somehow silence the hateful words that kept echoing in her brain. *Mountaineer, mountaineer, mountaineer. A twang to her voice... No sense of fashion...*

She wanted to deal with it when she got home; there she'd either give way to tears or hurl something across the room.

She jumped into her car and cranked the engine. Automatically her eyes shot to the upper window, and for a moment her hand froze on the steering wheel. Anna Lee was standing in the window, her face pressed to the glass as she peered down at Laurel with a smirk of contempt. The round lips spread wider, and Laurel could see she was laughing.

Laurel stared for a moment, unable to hear the laughter, but she knew how it would sound. Bitter and mocking.

Anna Lee had obviously heard the conversation between her mother and Matt. Now, for the first time since Laurel had known her, she had found something to amuse Anna Lee. But it was not normal, healthy laughter. It was the kind of cruel laughter that came at someone else's expense.

Laurel lifted her hand and waved lightly, as though unaware of Anna Lee's mockery. Then she focused on backing the car out and steering it carefully down the narrow drive.

Pride forced her to retain her composure until she was out of Anna Lee's sight. But once she turned onto the highway, she found that her anger had slipped to the back of her mind, replaced by something more disturbing. Madeline's haughty behavior and cruel words had cut Laurel; but she was more pained by the knowledge that Anna Lee was amused, even pleased, that her mother's vicious words had almost reduced Laurel to tears.

How sad they are, Laurel thought grimly. *How very sad.*

Four

L aurel suffered through a troubled night. The humiliation dealt her by Mrs. Wentworth and Anna Lee had been compounded by the memory of her final confrontation with Ryan.

She had believed Ryan to be a wonderful, sincere man, until a co-worker thought it her duty to inform Laurel of his many affairs. He was a "love 'em and leave 'em" guy, unable to commit himself to one relationship, she was warned. Still, she tried to believe that was all in the past until Ryan broke a date, saying he had to take his mother to visit a friend. Disappointed, Laurel had called a girlfriend and they had gone to a new restaurant where she spotted Ryan and a beautiful blonde cozied up at a table in the corner.

At the time, Laurel had not been sophisticated enough to keep her cool, and she had charged up to the table to confront him.

"I didn't realize your mother was so young," Laurel had said in a voice that dripped sarcasm.

Caught in his lie, Ryan had retaliated with anger. He had excused himself from his date and he and Laurel had continued their argument outside. He said many hurtful things to her, but one particular comment had remained in her heart.

"You thought I was teasing you about being from the mountains," he lashed out, "but it really bugs me the way you talk and act and think."

Laurel had been stunned; she had no idea he had resented so many things about her. Like Madeline, he had considered her a mountaineer.

Now, as she stood before the kitchen window, staring out at a blue sky, she wondered if the Wentworths were secretly irritated as Ryan had been. She closed her eyes for a moment. Her job was to help Anna Lee; that was all that really mattered.

Resigned to that conclusion, she turned to her bedroom to dress for a new day. However, her movements were slow and sluggish, so that she was almost late for her appointment with the dunking machine.

Laurel headed toward the dunking seat, ready to take the plunge for those who paid to play. Her mood improved as she glanced around, feeling the excitement of the fair take hold. Booths were bursting with homebaked goods and crafts, while the smell of cotton candy wafted on the summer morning. In addition to the booths and food, the volunteer firefighters had come up with what they considered a splendid way of making money—a dunking booth featuring teachers from grades one through twelve.

Laurel had accepted the challenge good-naturedly, determined to do her part in raising money for the firemen this year. She had come prepared, dressed in jeans, a sweatshirt, and flip-flops, lugging a shopping bag with a change of clothes. She was scheduled to go first, so she handed her bag to Mable, working the ticket booth, and climbed the narrow ladder. Once she settled onto her precarious seat, she gave the crowd a lofty bow. In response, volunteers in adjacent booths laughed and gave her a spatter of applause.

As her eyes moved over the crowd, she spotted her grandmother at once. A crowd was gathering to watch the seventh-grade teacher get dunked.

"Have fun," Granny called from the sidelines, her little face struggling with the laughter she tried to suppress.

"I will," Laurel said, making a face.

The sunny morning vibrated with the activity of the fair, and Laurel breathed a deep sigh. At least this would take her mind off the Wentworths.

There was a small fee for the three balls participants would throw at the bulls-eye to dunk Laurel. If anyone wanted to make a larger contribution, a sign invited them to do so.

She had been watching Toby Hankins drop a handful of coins into the bucket for the chance of dunking her. She recalled the afternoon she had made Toby stay after school and clean blackboards as punishment for putting a lizard down Amy Townsend's collar. She had scolded him severely, but she thought he had recovered. Still...she braced herself for the cold water.

"Hey, Toby," she called to him. "Bet you can't do it."

An impish grin tilted his freckled face as he rolled up his sleeves and recklessly hurled one ball after another with fiendish delight. Laurel held her breath, waiting. The balls whacked and rolled off center as Toby quickly exhausted his change and trudged off with a scowl.

She relaxed. Dunking her was not going to be such an easy feat after all, she decided smugly. With each ball that was tossed, her seat remained intact; she joked with the contestants, mostly former students. As her confidence grew, she loosened up even more. She was having fun...until she spotted Matt Wentworth.

Actually, it had been the whoop of delight from one of the firefighters that had attracted her attention. "Why, thank you, sir. You're very generous," he said to Matt.

Matt was standing at the bucket, dropping dollar bills. Apparently, they were big bills, judging from the glow on the faces of those managing the money.

She caught her breath, recalling the words she had heard from his mother. A mountaineer! Her pride suddenly retaliated, and words rolled recklessly from her lips.

"Why, suh, you ain't gonna dunk a little mountaineer like me, is you?" she taunted.

The mocking challenge had been issued to him, and there was no backing down. If she expected a laugh, or even an amused grin from him, she was in for a surprise.

Anger suddenly clouded his face as her words hit the mark, and she bit her lip. She had gone too far, and yet she felt as though her remark had freed her from the dark mood that had claimed her since leaving his house yesterday.

The crowd began to part like the Red Sea as Matt picked up the three balls and walked to the pitching line. Whispers flitted over the intrigued audience, while Laurel drew a shaky breath. The blue eyes pinned her and a confident grin lit his suntanned face.

She watched him grip the ball and rock back on his left foot while his left leg curled in a wind-up. The ball zinged through the air, slamming dead center onto the target. The platform dissolved as Laurel fell into the water.

When she finally fought her way to the surface, the crowd was ecstatic, roaring with laughter. An arm shot out, offering assistance as she awkwardly climbed out, trying in vain to smooth down her rumpled, water-logged jeans. The arm belonged to Matt, whose face was only inches away as water cascaded from her face and body.

"Thanks," she mumbled. Her cheeks burned with humiliation as she disengaged her arm and trudged toward the dressing room, with the crowd's laughter dulled by the slosh of water in her clothes.

Somehow she managed to get to the dressing room and shed her wet clothes in private. Once she had towel-dried her hair and donned fresh clothes, however, she began to have second thoughts about her taunting remark.

Matthew Wentworth could not be held responsible for the actions of his mother or sister. And yet, deep in her heart, she realized it wasn't just the "mountaineer" term that bothered her; it was Madeline Wentworth's reference to his other girlfriends in Atlanta. No doubt, he had girlfriends wherever he went; for that reason, Laurel was determined not to be added to his list of conquests. Again, the memory of Ryan's words returned to haunt her as she stood before the mirror in the dressing room, staring at her damp hair, swept into a ponytail. Looking at her reflection, she tried to assess herself honestly. Thoughts of Ryan, and now Matt, demanded honesty.

She stared at her face, pale from the cold water. Her lashes, still wet, accented the blue eyes tinged with gray. Her features looked small and delicate in the bright light, and her fresh jeans and pink and white striped T-shirt molded gently to her slim frame. She was grateful that her weight was not a problem and that she had never been bothered with acne. Yet she was certain that she must look plain compared to the sophisticated beauties in Atlanta. Matthew Wentworth had to date gorgeous women there, social types who measured up to his mother's expectations.

She sighed, feeling yesterday's dark mood sweep over her again. *I won't get downhearted,* she promised herself. *It isn't worth it. This is supposed to be a happy weekend.*

Holding that thought uppermost in her mind, she gathered her belongings and cracked the door.

The crowd's attention was now centered on Ted Fisher, taking his turn on the dunking machine. She cracked the door wider, scanning the laughing faces for Matt. He was nowhere in sight. Now that he'd had his fun, he had probably gone on to another attraction. It was safe to sneak out.

Breathing a sigh of relief, she decided to weave through the crowd to the cotton candy machine. It had always been one of her favorite treats, and the opportunity to sample cotton candy did not come often.

"Give me the biggest cotton candy you have, Charlie," she called, as Charlie, the school janitor, spun out the pink, cone-shaped fluff.

She dug into her jeans for a dollar, paid a grinning Charlie, then stuck out her tongue to sample the gooey sweetness.

"Mmmm," she said aloud, closing her eyes to relish another mouthful.

"A mountaineer who likes cotton candy!"

She jumped abruptly at the voice, just behind her left ear. The hand holding the cotton candy had dipped forward, brushing her face. When she turned, she met Matt's blue eyes over the wisp of cotton candy dangling from her nose.

His remark had been spoken in a tone that hinted of anger; but now, as his eyes swept her face and T-shirt, decorated in pink, he began to chuckle.

"Well," she said, lifting a hand to swipe at the mess, "you're definitely out to get me today."

"I'm just having fun. Fairs are supposed to be fun," he said, extending a clean linen handkerchief to her.

"Yes, they are," she snapped, raking the gooey mess from her face and T-shirt. In her awkwardness, another puff landed in her hair. "It's no use," she cried, turning to toss the cotton candy in the nearest trash bin.

He looked down at her with humor gleaming in his blue eyes and a little grin that did strange things to her senses. Her impulse was to turn and run, as fast as she could. She knew, in spite of everything, that she was on the brink of falling for Matt Wentworth. She couldn't imagine a worse mistake.

"Now what's wrong?" he asked. "You've impressed me as someone who enjoys good wholesome fun, but you suddenly look as though you hate the world."

"Not the world, just the cold water," she said, returning the handkerchief. "Thanks."

"You're welcome," he said with that amused grin still playing over his face.

Knowing that laughter was generally the best antidote to an embarrassing situation, she dug into her brain for a bit of humor. "Well, Mr. Wentworth, when you mentioned attending a private school, you didn't tell me you were their star baseball player!"

"Made All-State. How did you know?"

She nodded suspiciously. "Your wind-up was a dead give away, not to mention the accuracy of that first pitch. How could you be so cruel?" she asked. But a smile inched up her cheeks.

He was so good-natured and pleasant that Laurel found it difficult to stay mad at him. But then why should she? He had given her no reason to be angry. If she would admit the truth to herself, she knew she was angry with her inability to control her own feelings. At the moment, for example, her heart was booming like the drum in the school band, which had begun to play on the opposite side of the park.

"This is a nice little fair," he said, as they sauntered past a booth featuring corn shuck dolls and white oak baskets. The quilt booth was just ahead, and Laurel knew Granny would be perched on a stool, hawking the quilts.

Laurel glanced around, spotting the pizza booth located on the opposite side of the park. She looked up at Matt. "What do you say we get a drink at the pizza booth?" she asked.

"Great. Do you like pizza?" he asked, shoving his hands into the pockets of his jeans. He was wearing a golf shirt, which stretched across his broad shoulders and tapered to a slim waist. It was mint green, her favorite color.

"Do I like pizza?" she repeated. "In my opinion, it's the next best thing to cotton candy."

"Then why don't we see if the pizza is as good as the cotton candy? Only do try and hit your mouth this time." He laughed again, and she joined in, unable to keep a straight face.

Her eyes lifted to the beautiful sky, a serene blue with only a few baby clouds scattered about. She decided to forget yesterday and have a good time. She had never been able to stay mad for long.

"I will definitely hit my mouth this time," she promised, running a hand over her damp hair. She hadn't even put fresh make-up on, but it was too late to worry about it.

"You look fine," he said, grinning down at her.

"Oh well," she shrugged, "what's a wet head and freezing skin in the interest of a new fire hose?"

They both laughed and followed their noses to the spicy smell of pepperoni and yeasty crust. They ordered Cokes and pizza slices and sat down at the nearest bench.

A few stares were beginning to follow them, and Laurel knew it was just a matter of time until "Who is he?" would be whispered around. "He's my student's brother," she would reply if asked. She thought of Anna Lee, wishing she could have come. The poor girl needed to have fun; that was part of her problem.

"What's Anna Lee doing today?" she asked. She regretted the question as soon as it was asked, for Matthew's pleasant smile disappeared.

"Nothing. I offered to bring her down here, but she prefers to lounge in her room, watching television and eating. Lou is staying at the house this weekend while Mother is in Atlanta."

"I didn't know she was going," Laurel said casually.

"She just decided yesterday. She called for the company jet to come pick her up."

"Must be nice," Laurel said lightly, then glanced at Matt, who frowned slightly. "Sorry."

"She suffers from migraines," he continued smoothly. "In the past months, each attack has become worse, and I'm afraid she doesn't have the right medication. I suggested she see her doctor."

Laurel bit her lip, regretting her sarcasm. If Mrs. Wentworth were in pain, it would explain her rudeness to a point. Or at least it would be easier to make excuses for her.

"I'm sorry. How long has she been troubled with the headaches?"

"For years. About yesterday...," he paused, finishing the last bite of pizza. "You obviously heard what Mother said."

Laurel looked away, desperately wishing she had not made that ridiculous comment before he dunked her. "Let's just forget it," she said, lifting her cup to her lips for a mouthful of crushed ice.

"Let's not forget it! I'd like you to understand that I make my own decisions, and I choose my own friends. Mother likes to try and intervene, but she rarely changes my mind."

Laurel turned and studied him curiously. He looked and spoke like a man who knew his own mind. She doubted that his mother, or anyone else, would sway him once that mind was set.

"I believe you," she said, tossing her cup in the trash bin. "It doesn't matter anyway. You and I travel in different circles. We aren't likely to cross paths to the extent of causing your mother concern."

His blue eyes darkened as he tilted his head to look down into her face. He had opened his mouth to respond when suddenly Granny's familiar voice interrupted.

"There you are!" She was speaking to Laurel, of course, and yet her eyes were fixed on Matt as she openly surveyed him from head to toe.

"Yes, here I am," Laurel quipped. "Still wet behind the ears."

Granny laughed, though her eyes never budged from Matt's face.

61

"Matt," Laurel said on a deep sigh, "I'd like to introduce my grandmother, Betsy Hollingsworth, who happens to be the best cook in the county. That's why those blue ribbons are dangling from her pockets."

"It's a pleasure to meet you," Matt said, giving Granny a warm smile. "Maybe I should go in search of the food that won those ribbons. I'd love to sample your cooking."

Granny turned to Laurel. She had that funny little smile on her face, even though her hazel eyes held an expression of caution. The woman had already figured out who Matt was; the introduction was merely a formality now.

"Granny, this is Matthew Wentworth."

Granny nodded slowly then turned to Matt again. "How do you do?"

"I'm fine, thank you. This is a wonderful fair, isn't it?"

"Yes, it is." Granny hesitated, and Laurel waited for some remark designed to put the city slicker in place. To her astonishment, Granny did just the opposite. "If you're interested in sampling my cooking, why don't you come around for lunch tomorrow?"

Laurel's intake of breath was clearly audible to Matt who glanced at her briefly before nodding at Granny.

"Why, thank you. Are you coming, Laurel?"

"Well," she bit her lip, "I have my Sunday school class tomorrow morning and—"

"My invitation was for after church, Laurel," Granny said with a sly little grin. "Matt, do you go to church?"

"As a matter of fact, I do. I always attended services with my grandmother when I was living in Chattanooga."

Laurel rolled her eyes, although neither seemed to take

notice. Betsy Hollingsworth absolutely glowed as she absorbed that last tidbit of information. Laurel looked from her grandmother to Matt and realized the situation was clearly out of her hands. Granny had made up her mind to check this guy out, and he seemed perfectly willing to accommodate her. Laurel swallowed, aware there was no way to dodge the cozy little get-together Granny had planned.

"Then you two can come by after church," Granny stated matter-of-factly, the subject obviously closed. She whirled on her Keds and dashed after one of her friends, her red shirttail flapping above her jeans.

"What a cute little woman," Matt said, staring after her.

"She's one of a kind. Look," Laurel frowned, "she also has a way of putting people on the spot, as she did you just now. Please don't feel you have to be accommodating. If you want to decline, I can simply tell her you had to return to Atlanta."

"But I don't have to return to Atlanta."

Her eyes slid up to his face, and she met pure amusement glinting in his blue eyes.

She took a deep breath. "Do you really want to come to church?"

"Of course I do. And then I want to come to your grandmother's house for the best cooking in the county." He glanced at his watch. "I only wish I didn't have to run." He looked back at her. "If I'd known the community fair was this much fun, I wouldn't have lined up workers to come to the house this afternoon."

"Say hello to Anna Lee for me," Laurel said, shoving her hands into her pockets.

"I will." He winked. "See you tomorrow."

CHAPTER

Five

❧

Sunshine spilled over the steeple of the white clapboard community church as the crowd gathered for the Sunday morning service. As folks settled into their seats, making comments to their neighbors, a door opened at the front of the sanctuary. Laurel entered, trailed by a group of exuberant children.

She glanced casually around the church, noting that Matt was nowhere in the crowd. Her eyes moved to the third row from the front, finding her grandmother, who had turned to talk to Millie seated behind her.

Quickening her steps, Laurel made her way to her grandmother's pew, trying to squelch a feeling of disappointment as she sidestepped Granny's little feet encased in modest black pumps.

Laurel took her seat, smoothing her skirt around her. She wore an A-line dress, with tiny pastel flowers spread over a cream silk background. She ventured a glance at her grandmother, smiling as though nothing were wrong, nothing at all.

"You look awfully pretty this morning," Granny said.

"Thanks. So do you."

Laurel reached for a hymnal, feeling a bit embarrassed about Matt's absence. No doubt, Granny had gone to extra trouble for today's meal, thinking Matt would be present. She could imagine Granny ironing her best lace tablecloth and...

"Excuse me," a male voice whispered.

Laurel glanced toward the aisle where Matt, nodding politely to her grandmother, was turning into their pew. He was wearing a navy sports coat over a crisp white shirt and conservative tie. The tan slacks and navy leather loafers looked casual, yet Laurel knew, having lived in Atlanta, that the price of his clothing would astound most of the congregation.

Her eyes flew back to the song book, then to the song director coming to the podium. She gave Matt a quick smile as he settled into the vacant seat beside her.

Millie gasped behind her; no doubt, she would have some interesting news for the post office patrons this week. That one gasp seemed to set off a groundswell of whispered speculation.

"Good morning," he whispered.

"Good morning." There was a raspy sound to her voice, for in addition to Matt seated beside her, and Millie whispering behind her, she could hear Tommy Tailor who only spoke in shouts.

"Who's that man with teacher?"

A distinct "Hush" answered him while some giggles ricocheted in the background. Laurel fought an urge to turn around and glare.

To her enormous relief, John Williams, the song director, had announced the number of the opening hymn, and there was a rustle of pages. Matt made no move to pick up a hymnal; he obviously intended to share hers, an interesting concept, since she couldn't carry a tune. Her singing became a joke when she forgot how badly she sounded and lost herself in the song.

She swallowed, flipping through the pages.

"You passed it." His breath ruffled the wispy curl on her cheek. "It's 209," he whispered.

She stared at the page number, flipping backward. Locating the page, she forced a casual smile to her face and turned to thank him. A warm smile answered her.

"All stand. We'll sing the first and last verses," John's voice boomed out.

Laurel glanced at Granny, holding her song book confidently, singing in her usual soprano as though this morning was no different from all the other Sundays.

"What a friend we have in Jesus...," Matt's voice rose and fell smoothly, mingling in with those around her. He sang the song as though he knew it well. Laurel joined in, as quietly as possible. At the chorus, she moved her head a fraction, casually measuring Granny's expression. The little woman was looking directly at the choir, her expression serene.

Laurel followed her gaze to the faces in the choir. No one seemed to be staring at her and Matt, and she silently scolded herself for being so conceited, imagining she and Matt were the center of attention.

As voices swelled over the church in that familiar hymn, Laurel began to relax. As always, the feeling of being in God's house, singing hymns, and listening to the pastor's message brought a sense of peace.

She joined in the song, giving Matt a brighter smile. She

relaxed as she forced herself to listen to the reassuring words of the song and stopped thinking of herself. As for worrying about the people's reaction to Matt, what did it matter if he had more money than anyone else? He certainly had not flaunted his wealth; if anything, he had tried to conceal it. Rather than getting so uptight over his presence in church, she should appreciate his making the effort to attend.

By the time the hymn was finished and everyone took their seats, her nerves settled and she began to enjoy the service.

Later, as the crowd dispersed after the benediction, Millie almost knocked Widow Bentley flat as she scrambled to catch up with them.

"Betsy, heard your quilt won the blue ribbon!" Millie squeaked, while staring at Matt.

"I'm over here, Millie," Granny said dryly. "Have you met Matt Wentworth?"

"Why, no. I haven't," Millie cooed, as Matt preceded to charm her into a state of giggles.

Afterward, the congregation migrated toward Laurel and Granny like bees flocking to honey. While the people were sincere in their welcome to Matt, there was obvious interest in his association with Laurel.

When they finally made their way to the parking lot, Matt turned to her. "Are you riding with your grandmother?"

"I hope not," she laughed, watching Granny's little white car scatter gravel and quickly disappear. "No, I have my own car. If you want to follow me to Granny's house..."

"I'll do that," he smiled, opening her car door for her.

From the corner of her eye, she saw little Tommy being collared by his father while he squirmed and yelled about wanting to talk to teacher. *What a morning!*

She slid into the front seat, stacking her books and purse beside her. "Well, see you there."

He smiled down at her. "I'm looking forward to your grandmother's meal."

"So am I."

She turned the key in the ignition and started the engine, watching through the rearview mirror as he headed for his car. He nodded politely to those he passed, and at one point, stopped to open the door for a lady encumbered with boxes. Was he always so polite, so kind? She remembered that he had spent years with a woman he described as the most wonderful person in the world. Obviously, she had instilled some admirable traits in him. Or perhaps he had learned from his father. She found herself wondering exactly what kind of man Matt's father had been.

Guiding her car past the crowd, she waved to the families she passed as she drove out of the parking lot. Was it her imagination or was there a new twinkle in every eye as they looked at her? She fought a twinge of annoyance; she'd never liked everyone knowing her business. Granny said she was just like her father in that respect.

She took a deep breath, adjusting her rearview mirror. She could see the Jeep pulling out behind her. Quickly, she averted her eyes to the road ahead, determined to stop peering at him. And yet it was hard not to stare because she kept seeing something more appealing than his good looks. Intelligence and sensitivity flashed from those blue eyes, and a look of keen interest when he turned those eyes on her. She fought against an underlying hope that his attention counted for more than just a friendship.

Turning onto the main street that led out of town, she told herself for the hundredth time that she had no future with Matt Wentworth. In her school teaching vernacular, he was a no-no. They had nothing in common and even if they did, she already knew what his mother's reaction would be. *So what are we doing?* she wondered, feeling the frustration mount.

He was only looking for friendship, obviously. Why couldn't she leave it at that? Well, she could; would. And he must do the same.

She pressed harder on the accelerator as she hit the open road, while continuing the mental battle. He was Anna Lee's older brother, a stranger here, a nice man who had gone to church and was now coming home to Granny's for Sunday dinner, as many others had done.

Soon, the green fields, ripe with summer grass and vegetable crops, had zipped past, and Granny's frame house came into view behind the white picket fence.

Laurel slowed down, giving her signal, checking the rearview mirror. Matt still trailed behind her.

Granny's car was already in the garage. Laurel knew when her grandmother had scooted on ahead of them that she was thinking of getting a head start on lunch plans.

Laurel negotiated the narrow drive, pulling up far enough to give Matt space to park. She cut the engine, reached for her purse, and hopped out, waiting.

He parked and got out, looking concerned. "You should slow down. That little car could go into a skid on one of those sharp curves back there."

"I suppose. But you see, my car and I have an agreement. I'll take care of her if she'll take care of me. So far, we've had no problems." She paused, seeing that he was not amused. "You're right. I should slow down," she said, more seriously.

Matt turned to survey the landscape. "It's beautiful here," he said.

"Yeah." Laurel shaded her eyes and scanned the tranquil meadows surrounding the house. "This land has been in our family for over a hundred years."

"You're kidding."

"Nope. My ancestors came in a wagon train from Virginia, looking for land to homestead. They found this spot, here in the shadow of the Smokies, where they could raise crops, hunt game, and graze a few head of cattle."

"Come in," Granny called from the screen door. She wandered onto the front porch and leaned down to remove a dead petal from a scarlet geranium.

Matt followed Laurel up the porch steps, then paused to touch one of the oak rockers. "I'd like to have some chairs like these for our place."

Laurel found it difficult to imagine either Madeline Wentworth or Anna Lee reclining on a porch to appreciate the view. Yet it seemed to Laurel that a healthy dose of nature might do wonders for them. At least, it would be a start in the right direction.

"I can tell you where to get some," Granny offered. "Harold Birdsong, a neighbor just up the road, makes sturdy rockers. He puts his heart and soul into his work. I don't think you'll find better chairs."

"I'm sure I won't," Matt said, examining the smooth wood.

"Still, you might want to ride up to Gatlinburg to the arts

and crafts community," Granny said, studying the rocker. "You can find anything from wood working to metal spinning up there."

"You'd love that place!" Laurel spoke up. "It's an authentic community of working craftspeople who chose to live in the kind of setting that inspires their work. Some of the businesses have been passed from one generation to another, while others were started by people who left boring jobs to live here and do work that captures their heart and soul."

Matt listened thoughtfully. "Sounds intriguing. Could you go along, help me find it?"

"Oh, it's easy to find," Laurel said, evading the invitation.

Matt picked up on her hesitation and turned to Granny. "Laurel was just telling me how your family homesteaded here. That's very interesting."

Granny nodded. "This farm was originally three hundred acres, but my grandfather sold off a hundred acres, and my father sold more. After my husband died, I had to let most of the land go to help educate my sons. They had decided they didn't want to farm, so there seemed no point in trying to hang on. Now I'm down to only a few acres, and it's almost more than I can take care of."

Matt stared at her. "Would you want to sell some land along the road?"

"No, she wouldn't," Laurel replied quickly.

Granny frowned. "Sometimes I think about it, when I wish for new carpeting throughout the house, or maybe a fancy little patio out back. But no, not yet."

She opened the door and motioned them inside. "Laurel may have told you her father died years ago; my middle son, Frank,

71

chose city life, and Bill, my youngest, wanted a military career. Everyone has to choose what they feel is right for them."

Matt paused on the porch, glancing past the neat yard and picket fence to the meadows that stretched to the foothills. "No city I've seen offers this kind of beauty," he said, "but then I was raised in cities. I suppose we gravitate toward something different."

Laurel stared at him, thinking he may have spoken the reason for his interest in her.

"I've been happy to stay right here," Granny smiled. "Sometime, if you like, I'll show you around. The original corn-crib and springhouse are still here; we had hoped to save the first cabin, but a fire claimed it in 1940. This house was built over fifty years ago. It's something of a relic," she winked at Laurel, "like me."

"Oh, Granny, you're far from being a relic." They entered the living room and Laurel nudged Matt. "She could probably out-run me if we ever had a foot race."

He chuckled at the remark while his eyes slipped over the living room, moving on to the dining room table.

As Laurel suspected, Granny had pulled her finest lace cloth from the bottom shelf of the buffet, along with her best china and silver. The table was neatly set; silver gleamed and crystal sparkled. A bud vase held two perfect red roses from Granny's fertile flower garden out back.

Matt turned to Laurel. "If the food tastes as good as it smells, I know why she's considered the best cook in the county."

Granny grinned at Matt. "Shed your coat and get comfortable while I kick off these heels for another week."

"Here, let me take your coat," Laurel offered.

"Thanks."

He shrugged out of his blazer and handed it to her. Laurel noticed that his hands were strong and masculine; he wore a college ring. As she stood close to him, breathing his cologne, feeling his eyes upon her, she felt another pang of nervousness. Her eyes drifted up to his face, which was tilted slightly, looking at her with an expression she couldn't read.

She turned away, heading for the closet. As she reached for a coat hanger, the enticing smell of his cologne wafted up, a spicy fragrance that reminded her of evergreens on a cool autumn day. The aroma was subtle yet nice, very nice. She closed the closet door and looked across the room.

With his arms crossed over his starched white shirt, he was looking around the living room filled with family pictures and Granny's handiwork.

What is Matt Wentworth doing here? she thought suddenly.

The question had been nagging all morning. He didn't belong with them any more than she belonged at the Wentworth house.

"You two take a seat," Granny called from the kitchen. "The meal is warming in the oven; I'll have it on the table in a jiffy."

"Let me help," Laurel offered, crossing the living room to the kitchen. "I appreciate you going to so much trouble," Laurel said under her breath, as she surveyed the many pots and pans brimming with aromas that made her mouth water.

"It's no trouble. I love to cook for my family," she said, grabbing a gloved pot holder from the cabinet. She opened the oven and pulled out a huge roasting pan.

Laurel peered over her shoulder, wondering what delight to expect as Granny lifted the lid to reveal a juicy roast garnished

73

with tiny potatoes and glazed carrots.

"What can I do?" Matt asked from the doorway.

Laurel had opened her mouth to refuse his help, but something stopped her. Perhaps it was the boyish delight in his eyes as he took in the cozy kitchen. She realized suddenly that this experience was unique for him, and so she tried to think up a job to make him feel at home.

"After I fill the glasses with tea, you could take the pitcher to the table," Laurel said, then hesitated. "You do drink tea?"

"Like all good Southern boys!"

When everything had been arranged on the table, Matt hurried forward to pull back the chairs for both women. Granny's brown eyes sparkled up at Matt as she settled into her chair.

Watching this, Laurel smothered a sigh. Sometime next week, Granny was sure to go on about Matthew Wentworth's manners.

"You can take a seat at the end of the table, Matt," Granny said, spreading a linen napkin across her lap. "I'll say grace."

After Granny's prayer, simple yet eloquent, she began to pass the platters of food, and soon everyone was eating heartily.

"Try some of my green tomato relish." She looked at Laurel. "I sold out within five minutes yesterday."

"I like your fried green tomatoes even better," Laurel said.

Matt looked up. "Fried green tomatoes?"

Granny glanced at Matt. "Next time you come, I'll have fried green tomatoes."

Next time. That statement made Laurel uncomfortable; she hoped Matt didn't think they were being pushy, but the idea seemed to please him.

He was looking at Granny with a big smile. "I'll look forward to it, Mrs. Hollingsworth. This is absolutely the best food I've ever put in my mouth."

"Oh, come on," she waved the compliment aside. "Surely with all those restaurants in Atlanta, you've tasted better food than this."

"The best chef in town could take a lesson from you," he said, chewing slowly, obviously relishing every bite. "My grandmother in Chattanooga was a good cook until her last stroke. Now she has a housekeeper who does the cooking."

"How serious was the stroke?" Granny asked, concerned.

"Not life-threatening. And, thank God, her memory was not impaired."

"This is your paternal grandmother?" Laurel asked, recalling their previous conversation.

"Yes." He looked at Granny. "I think you'd like her. And I know she'd adore you."

"Maybe someday you can bring her up for a visit," Granny suggested. "I'd enjoy meeting her."

Matt frowned. "I'd like to, but...," he faltered, glancing from Granny to Laurel, "as Laurel may have told you, my mother is not an easy person to get along with. She and Grandmother Wentworth have never been close."

"But she could come visit *you*," Granny offered in the simple logic that usually evaded others when trying to solve a problem.

Matt brightened. "Yes, perhaps someday she could do that. She's a woman of faith, like you," he added quietly.

"Good. Maybe in time," Granny said gently, "your mother will see things differently."

Matt said nothing for a moment, as a tiny frown settled into

75

a groove between his brows. "I don't know. I've almost given up hope that my mother will ever change."

"Never give up hope," Granny smiled at him.

Matt smiled but said nothing more.

Granny pushed her chair back and looked from Matt to Laurel. "Save room for some apple pie."

Laurel touched her stomach. "I don't know..."

"Laurel, you can have a bite," Granny insisted, hurrying toward the kitchen.

Laurel shook her head in exasperation. "Over the years, if I'd let Granny talk me into sampling just a bite, I'd weigh two hundred pounds."

Matt's eyes swept her slender frame. "I'm sure weight has never been a problem for you."

Granny reappeared with three generous slabs of pie, oozing with cinnamon and apple juices.

"Will is coming next week," Granny announced, looking across at Laurel.

"Will?" Laurel smiled. "I haven't seen him in years. On his last trip home, I was teaching in Marietta. How is he?"

"He's doing very well! The publishing company he works for has asked him to do a picture book of Cades Cove."

"Wonderful!" Laurel exclaimed. She glanced at Matt. "Will—William Hargate—is a local boy who has a talent for photography." She looked back at Granny. "Will he be staying with you?"

"Reckon so. This is home to Will."

"Is he a relative?" Matt asked politely.

"Just one of my boys," Granny smiled. "Will was orphaned when he was fifteen. He lived with me until he finished high school. Then he went up to Knoxville, got a job, and put himself through the university. I'm proud of Will," she said, glancing back at Laurel. "He'll want to see you. He always asks about you." She glanced at Matt. "He's been in New York the past couple of years."

"How old is he?" Matt inquired.

Something in the tone of his voice piqued the interest of both women. Was his question purely conversational, or did he wonder if there might be something more than friendship between Will and Laurel?

"Will is," Granny paused, counting the years, "almost thirty, by now."

Matt nodded. "My age."

"He's a great guy," Laurel said, exchanging a smile with Granny. Laurel could never think of Will as more than a friend, but Granny claimed that Will had always been in love with Laurel.

"Well," Matt glanced at his watch and stood up. "As much as I hate to leave, I have to get back to Atlanta this afternoon." He looked from Laurel to Granny. "I can't thank you enough. The meal and the company were exceptional."

"Then come again," Granny beamed.

Laurel found herself at a loss for words. She realized she didn't want him to leave, that she had thoroughly enjoyed being with him.

He looked at Laurel. "I wish you luck with my sister this week, but of course you'll need a lot more than luck. You'll need a ton of patience."

77

"We'll make it," Laurel spoke with false confidence where the Wentworth women were concerned, but she tried to hide her frustration. "I'll get your coat."

As she hurried to the closet and reached for his blazer, Laurel's eyes slipped over the smooth dark linen set off by gold buttons. His cologne lingered on the jacket, and she took a deep breath, wanting to remember the fragrance in case she never saw him again. The idea brought a strange ache to her heart as she gripped the coat and headed for the front door, where Matt was saying goodbye to Granny.

Laurel handed him the coat and smiled. "Have a safe return."

He looked at her for several seconds before he tossed the coat over his arm and nodded. "Thanks. And Mrs. Hollingsworth, thanks again for inviting me to church and to share your Sunday meal."

"You're most welcome." Granny looked him over thoughtfully.

"Well...goodbye," he said for the third time before he hurried toward his Jeep.

Laurel wasted no time getting to the dining room table to start clearing away the dishes. "I'll just help you clean up and then I'll be on my way."

"Hold it," Granny said, placing a hand on Laurel's shoulder.

Laurel paused, her arms loaded with dishes, her eyes drifting across to her grandmother.

"He's the nicest young man I've met since I met your grand-father," Granny said.

Laurel stared at her for a silent moment before she turned and trudged to the kitchen with Granny hot on her heels.

"Well, it's the truth," Granny defended her statement.

Laurel busily unloaded dishes at the sink then hurried back to the dining table for more. "Yes, he's a gentleman, Granny. But don't go getting any ideas."

"Ideas about what?"

Laurel's eyes shot to her. "You know what. Ideas about...him and...me."

Granny shrugged lightly, turning her attention toward the table. "You're the one who brought that up. Not me."

The sound of the Jeep's engine faded into the distance, and Laurel turned dismal eyes toward the window.

Was she the only one who was getting such ideas? If so, she had to stop thinking like that. She hadn't a chance with Matt Wentworth. She had made that statement to herself a dozen times since meeting him. So...why wasn't her heart getting the message?

Laurel found herself dreading her Monday morning trip to Raven Ridge more than she had dreaded that first interview. Dressed in Keds, a floral skirt, and sleeveless pink blouse, she hurried up the broad stone steps and lifted the brass knocker. As it thudded into the morning stillness, she took a deep breath, shifting the load of books in her arms.

She was relieved when Lou answered the door.

"Good morning," Lou smiled. "Come in."

"Good morning, Lou." Laurel smiled as her eyes moved over the quiet hall. "Are the others asleep?"

"Mrs. Wentworth is still in Atlanta, but Anna Lee is dressed and waiting."

"She is?" Surprised by this news, Laurel hurried to the living room, curious about her student.

Anna Lee sat on the sofa, flipping through the pages of a book Laurel had left. "When are we going up on the parkway like you promised?" she asked in greeting.

Laurel placed her books and purse on the table, then straightened her back and studied Anna Lee. She wore another sweat-suit, one less wrinkled than before, and her hair was neatly combed. The dull expression that had filled her eyes the previous week was gone; instead, Laurel could see a spark of interest, and that pleased her immensely.

The memory of Friday afternoon and the image of Anna Lee's smirking face threatened, but Laurel was determined to forget the incident and get on with her life. She took a deep breath and glanced at the picture book. It was a new week. Why not start with a clean slate?

"As a matter of fact," Laurel said, taking a seat opposite her, "I was hoping we could go up on the parkway later in the week, weather permitting."

"Good! I'm getting bored."

"You are? Then take a look at what I've brought."

Laurel reached for a book she had discovered among her treasure trove. It was a history book that deviated from the textbook style of teaching, and was one her students had found interesting.

"Excuse me," Lou spoke from the doorway. "What did you want me to plan for lunch?"

Anna Lee shrugged. "Whatever she wants."

Laurel couldn't help staring at Anna Lee for a moment before turning to Lou. "Let's see. What about a baked lunch?" Laurel suggested. "A heavy meal puts me to sleep."

"Baked chicken?" Lou suggested.

"That sounds wonderful."

"I don't care." Anna Lee seemed indifferent as she sat with her head lowered over the book again.

Curiously, Laurel glanced at the source of her interest. She was studying a picture of native wildlife found in the Smoky Mountains. *What has changed her?* Laurel wondered. She was tempted to compliment Anna Lee on her behavior, but her instincts told her not to make an issue of it, not then, but rather to act as though the girl's behavior was perfectly normal.

This turned out to be the best decision, Laurel realized, as she got to know Anna Lee better. The girl hated discussing her innermost feelings and thoughts with adults; like most girls her age, she was painfully self-conscious, certain that everyone was watching everything she said and did.

The morning passed pleasantly with Anna Lee showing more interest in her school work than she had displayed the previous week.

When Lou announced lunch, Laurel came quickly to her feet, relieved that Madeline was still in Atlanta. *Ah, a peaceful lunch at last,* she thought with a sigh. Laurel still hadn't forgotten Friday's incident when Mrs. Wentworth had referred to her as a "mountaineer," warning Matt that he should not add her to his conquests. Still, Laurel tried to push the memory from her mind. This was a new day, and she was just grateful for the pleasant change in Anna Lee.

Laurel arrived home and was unlocking the door when the phone began to ring. The small, two-bedroom cottage she rented was a source of pride to her, for she had decorated it exactly to suit her taste, utilizing local arts and crafts mixed with handmade furniture from the area.

She raced across the hardwood floor of the living room to reach the wall phone in the kitchen.

"Hello," she said, breathlessly.

"Hi, this is Matt."

"Hi." She was taken by surprise, and for a moment she was at a total loss for words.

"I was just calling to see how your day went."

"Anna Lee was a model student today," she answered truthfully. "I feel good about her progress."

"Glad to hear it. I wasn't sure what you'd be dealing with. Laurel," he hesitated for a moment, "I had a talk with my mother before she left today. I hope she'll be more agreeable."

"Matt, please don't feel you have to come to my defense. I don't want to cause problems."

"You aren't causing any problems, you're trying to solve a few. My mother is still trying to pull herself together after losing Dad. She has a hard time adjusting to changes in her life or her routine."

"I know it's been rough for all of you. I just don't want to create any..." she groped for a word. "Confusion."

"You won't. Look, I'd like to see some of the arts and crafts that we discussed on Sunday. I have an idea about using some of their work. Would you be willing to show me that community you mentioned?"

Laurel bit her lip. If she had a pet project, it was helping the talented mountain people find markets for their work. "I suppose I could."

"How about Saturday?" he asked quickly. "Do you have plans?"

She hesitated. How could she gracefully refuse? How could she subject herself to another day with him, when she was already fighting an attraction that would lead nowhere?

"Well, what do you say?" he pressed.

She decided there was no way she could turn him down. It was exactly the kind of day she would enjoy, and if he purchased anything, it would help the local artists. So why not? She'd just have to keep a tight rein on her emotions.

"Sure. I'd like to go," she answered. "What time?"

"Why don't I pick you up around nine o'clock? I forgot to mention I'm a morning person; I get up with the sun. If that's too early for you..."

"No, that's fine."

"Great. Oh, by the way, I'd like to give you my telephone numbers here in Atlanta. In case there's an emergency with Anna Lee," he added tactfully.

"Good idea." She scrambled for the pencil and notepad on the kitchen counter and jotted down the numbers he gave her. She hoped there would never be the kind of emergency that would warrant having to call him in Atlanta.

"See you on Saturday," he said before hanging up.

She replaced the headset in its cradle and stared blankly at the sheer yellow curtains framing the window over the sink. Yesterday she had thought she might never see him again; yet within twenty-four hours, they had a date.

Was it his habit to come up every weekend to check on his family? Or did she have anything to do with it?

"I hate this horrible weather," Anna Lee burst out as Laurel entered the living room the next day. She was standing before the glass wall, glaring at the clouds.

Laurel looked from the sky to Anna Lee, thinking that her pupil's face was as stormy as the sky.

"Maybe we can find something else to do," Laurel suggested.

"Like what?" Anna Lee regarded her suspiciously.

"For starters, let's get some positive thoughts going here. A rainy day is great for reading."

"I don't want to read!" She turned and flopped on the sofa.

"Why not?" Laurel took a seat in the armchair opposite Anna Lee. "There are some wonderful books in the library."

Anna Lee dawdled with her hair, twirling a strand around her fingers. "Which ones do you call *wonderful?*" she mocked.

"Why don't we go see?"

She had spoken on impulse, but quickly decided it had been a good one. Anna Lee leaned forward, showing some interest.

"Maybe we could find some books that would relate to your school work and be fun to read."

"There aren't any books like that," Anna Lee said, watching Laurel carefully.

"I beg to differ with you. I can think of some wonderful stories about explorers and scientists and pioneers."

"I don't believe you!" While her words held a challenge, the frown had disappeared and her tone of voice was no longer an invitation to a fight.

"Then I guess I'll just have to prove my point. Grab an umbrella. But first we must ask your mother if it's okay to go to the library."

Laurel had spotted Madeline's black Mercedes parked in the drive this morning and knew she was back from Atlanta.

"You mean there's a library here?" Anna Lee had spoken as though they were stranded on the Sahara, but Laurel kept her tone light and pleasant in response.

"Of course! I think you'll be pleased by our variety of books. You see, when you live miles away from all of the city's entertainment, folks pitch in to help each other. We have a crafts fair every summer and a weekend festival in the fall to raise money for community projects. Last year we raised thousands of dollars for new books and videos for the public and school libraries."

Anna Lee stood, glancing toward the hallway. "I'll go up and tell Mother we're going."

She hurried off. Taking a deep breath, Laurel went in search of Lou.

She found her standing at the kitchen sink, washing dishes. "Lou, we won't be having lunch here today," Laurel said. "I'm taking Anna Lee to the library, and then I'll treat her to a salad at the cafe."

"Have a good day," Lou smiled. There was a look of compassion in the woman's dark eyes. Laurel suspected that Lou, too, had born the brunt of Madeline's sarcasm, and the woman appreciated the challenge Laurel faced with both Madeline and Anna Lee.

"Thanks, Lou. You, too!"

The library proved to be a source of delight for Anna Lee. Laurel could scarcely believe how little the girl knew about authors and titles. Later, Anna Lee confided the reason behind her lack of knowledge.

"My dad gave more money to our private school than anyone else. I never really had to do anything I didn't want to do."

Shocked by her statement, Laurel gently led Anna Lee into a

conversation that revealed even more distressing news. Anna Lee had been accorded many privileges, such as skipping tests and projects if she was sick. Laurel suspected that Anna Lee had been sick whenever it suited her. Furthermore, her school schedule was organized around family affairs and the frequent shopping trips she and her mother made, with the company jet at their disposal.

When the school administered the required competency test, the shock of Anna Lee's low scores had thrown both teachers and Madeline Wentworth into a frenzy about her future.

"Can we come back to the library sometime?" Anna Lee asked, as they returned to Laurel's car.

"Sure. We can go once a week, if your mother has no objections."

"She doesn't care," Anna Lee said in a toneless voice, as she got in the car and buckled her seat belt. "She only cares about her garden clubs and her snobby friends."

"She cares about you," Laurel said gently. "She went to a lot of trouble to get a tutor for you."

"She just doesn't want me to be an embarrassment to her this fall," Anna Lee sighed.

Laurel glanced quickly at Anna Lee, wondering if there was any truth to that. The girl picked up one of the library books and opened it. "You made a good choice of books," Laurel said, and smiled at her.

Anna Lee had chosen biographies of Amelia Earhart and Christopher Columbus. Laurel pondered the wide diversity between a woman flying and a man's sea voyage to the new world. She suspected the girl had a curious—perhaps even gifted—mind once someone inspired her to use it.

The rain that had held off all morning burst down from the skies in drenching sheets, slashing at their windshield so hard that Laurel could barely see the highway through the curtain of gray.

"I'm scared!" Anna Lee burst out. "I want to go home!"

"Don't be afraid. I've driven through rain storms before. Tell you what," Laurel said, pulling into the driveway of the community church, "we'll run in here until the rain lets up. This week is Bible school and—"

"What's Bible school?"

Laurel carefully negotiated her little car up the driveway to a side door. She stole a quick glance toward Anna Lee, who looked genuinely puzzled.

"Haven't you ever been to vacation Bible school in the summer?" Laurel asked.

"We don't go to church."

Laurel cut the engine and turned to Anna Lee. "In the summer, we set aside a week for the school children in which they have stories and crafts and games. It's a lot of fun," she smiled.

Anna Lee gave her that all-too-familiar look of doubt.

"Come on, grab your umbrella. You can see for yourself."

They made a dash through the rain to a side door, where Jimmy Barker rushed up, his mouth circled in cherry punch, his chubby little hands stained with magic markers.

"Laurel, Laurel," he squealed. "Come see the clown."

Anna Lee stared at him as though he were a cartoon character who had leaped from a television screen.

"Well, come on," Laurel tapped Anna Lee's shoulder, "let's go see the clown!"

❧

Anna Lee was still chuckling by the time they arrived back at the house.

"I wish we had Clarence the Clown at our school."

"It would be difficult to get Clarence to leave here." Laurel parked the car and turned the ignition off. "You see, Clarence is really Billy, a young man who is, well, a bit simpleminded. But we give him different jobs around town. His favorite job is dressing up and replaying the cartoon acts he watches on television."

Anna Lee stared at her. "Not really."

"Really," Laurel said, glancing at the house. "We've been gone all day. Your mother is probably wondering what happened."

Anna Lee gathered up her books and umbrella and reached for the door handle. She hesitated.

"What is it?" Laurel asked.

"I had a good time," she said shyly. When she turned back to Laurel, a tiny smile touched her lips.

"Thank you, Anna Lee, so did I."

As Laurel sat watching Anna Lee plod through the rain, a warm glow of joy spread over her. These were the rewards of teaching, Laurel decided, these special times when a student began to grow and develop in all the right ways.

$\mathscr{S}even$

aurel was humming a romantic ballad to herself as she turned up the driveway to Raven Ridge. Yesterday's rain was gone, and bright sunlight splashed down the mountaintops and spread a gold sheen over the valley.

She parked her car and hopped out, thinking that they would go over the various plants they would be seeing the next day up on the parkway. She knocked on the door and waited, a friendly greeting on her lips for Lou when she opened the door. It was not Lou who answered, but rather Madeline Wentworth. Dressed in dark slacks and shirt, she, too, looked dark and grim and thoroughly out of sorts.

"Good morning," Laurel said, attempting a friendly smile.

"Good morning," Madeline said curtly. "Anna Lee came down with a sore throat last night and was coughing this morning. I suggested she stay in bed today."

"Oh, I'm sorry," Laurel was about to mention their trip to the library, perhaps comment on Anna Lee's choice of books, when Madeline spoke again.

"I understand you two were out traipsing around in the rain!" She lifted a jeweled hand to check the condition of her hairdo. The short hair appeared to be lacquered to her head. "I would prefer you not take her out again when the weather is bad," Madeline instructed, her tone abrupt.

Laurel took a breath before she spoke. "It was not raining when we left and—"

"But you obviously expected rain; otherwise, she wouldn't have taken an umbrella."

"We used our umbrellas," Laurel answered calmly, "so I'm surprised that she got a sore throat."

"She told me," Madeline said, through narrowed eyes, "that you went to some clown show in the basement of a church. If the basement was damp, I expect that helped the sore throat along."

Laurel fell silent. There was nothing she could say. Yes, the basement was damp, but it never seemed to bother anyone else.

"Which brings up another point," Madeline said, tilting her head back to give Laurel the full benefit of her icy stare. "I do not allow my daughter to be dragged into churches. I have some definite ideas about religion, and I will decide when, or *if*, she goes to a church."

Laurel was astounded by her words. *The woman is a monster.* For Anna Lee's sake, Laurel felt compelled to make one point very clear.

"I didn't think you'd mind Anna Lee watching a children's program in church. She had a good time."

"Clarence the Clown," Madeline's voice mocked. "Is that your idea of a tutoring session?"

Laurel felt her temper mounting, wanting to leave before saying something she would regret. But first, she felt the need to make one more point, providing she could keep her voice calm enough to speak.

"Mrs. Wentworth," she spoke slowly, emphatically, "we spent most of our time at the library. I believe Anna Lee needs improvement in her library skills. In any case, the books she checked out are biographies relating to history. As for stopping at the church, we were merely waiting out the rain. I don't believe any harm was done," she said pointedly. "I've been tutoring her for almost two weeks, but yesterday was the first time I've seen her laugh."

Madeline merely shrugged.

"I hope she feels better soon," Laurel said.

"So do I. Plan to come back tomorrow unless you hear from us," Madeline said and slammed the door.

For several seconds, Laurel merely stared at the closed door. Then she turned and headed back to the car, thoroughly depressed. She decided to make a trip out to Granny's, hoping to improve her mood.

As soon as she turned into the driveway, Granny came out on the porch, grinning from ear to ear.

"Did you get one too?" she called.

"One what?" Laurel asked as she hopped out of the car and approached the porch.

Granny's brown eyes glowed with a special secret. "Come inside."

As they entered the living room, Granny pointed to a lush fern in a hanging basket displayed in the front window.

"Isn't it lovely?"

"Well, of course. But who—"

"Matt. Here, read the note."

Wide-eyed, Laurel reached for the small white card and read the message. "Thank you for a wonderful Sunday."

"How sweet," Laurel said, reading the message again before returning the card to Granny. Her eyes drifted back to the huge fern which did, indeed, add something special to Granny's small room. "That was very thoughtful."

"Fanny delivered it this afternoon. Maybe you'll be getting one."

"I didn't cook the meal." Laurel smiled, but then her smile faded as her thoughts returned to Matt's mother. "Granny, it's difficult for me to believe that this man, who sends a plant and a sweet message, is even related to Madeline Wentworth."

"Maybe the woman hasn't always been as hard or unfeeling. Or maybe something is causing her to behave the way she does."

"Something? Well, the death of her husband has thrown her into a depression, still...," Laurel's voice trailed away as she thought of Madeline and the way her eyes sometimes looked glazed, as though she had just taken medication.

"Just concentrate on Anna Lee. She needs you. It's hard to figure a woman like that with a son as nice as Matt. When is Matt coming back up?"

"He called last night. We're going to the arts and crafts community on Saturday."

"Good! And don't let that woman's bad behavior spoil things."

Laurel shook her head miserably. "Granny, she doesn't approve of her son seeing me."

"Phooey," Granny waved the matter aside. "He's a grown man, perfectly capable of making his own decisions. And so are you." Granny reached forward, patting Laurel's hand. "Just be your sweet self and go on about your life. Let God deal with Mrs. Wentworth."

Laurel shook her head. "How can God deal with Madeline Wentworth when she doesn't believe in God? Or she doesn't seem to. But you're right," Laurel conceded. "Only God can change that woman!" She leaned forward and kissed her grandmother's cheek. "You always make me feel better. What would I do without you?"

"I don't know," she replied with an impish little grin.

When Laurel arrived home, she found a fern, just like Granny's, waiting beside her door.

"Oh, Matt," she sighed, reaching for the card. *Looking forward to Saturday,* the message read.

Touched by his kindness, she vowed to forget Madeline's behavior. Granny was right; she should simply concentrate on Anna Lee, and maybe even Matt, and leave Madeline to God.

Cradling the huge fern, she unlocked the door just as the telephone rang. She placed the fern on a table and hurried to answer.

"Hi. It's me."

"Anna Lee! How are you feeling?" Laurel asked worriedly.

"I'm all right. Mother was just being mean. My throat was barely sore, and I only coughed a little. Are you coming tomorrow?" Her voice conveyed a tone of hope.

"Sure. Think you're up to hitting the books again?"

"Yeah, I could have today. Are we going on the field trip?"

Laurel chose her words carefully. "Let's wait until the weather improves a little bit more. Have you been reading your library books?"

"Mmm-hmmm. I want to know more about this Lindbergh woman."

Laurel smiled. "Okay. And we'll have a good week, Anna Lee." Laurel wondered if she were trying to convince Anna Lee or herself as they said goodbye and hung up.

She turned back to the fern, wondering where to hang it. *The window, of course.* Her eyes roamed idly over the well-used furnishings. She often described her decorating scheme as "early attic," with furnishings from her family and garage sales. All the gifts her students had given her were displayed throughout.

While the house was tiny—a living and dining room, small kitchen, two bedrooms, and a bath—she had put her own touch to the interior and made it feel homey.

She wandered to the window, smiling. *I'll put up a hook and hang it there.* She sank into the chair gazing at the fern. Matthew was a very thoughtful man.

Through the window she could see the Lewis children playing in their yard across the street. They were devising their own game from a half-deflated volleyball; yet they laughed and chased each other around in the joyous, carefree manner of children.

She thought of Anna Lee and wondered if she had ever felt that kind of joy or freedom.

For the rest of the week, Madeline did not put in an appearance at the lunch table or in the living room where Laurel and Anna Lee studied. Laurel was enormously relieved to be spared encountering her. Anna Lee's sore throat healed, and when they said goodbye on Friday, both Laurel and her student were in good spirits.

On Saturday morning, Laurel stood before the floor-length mirror on her door. With a critical eye she appraised herself from head to toe. She wore new leather Keds, stonewashed jeans, and a pale lavender sports shirt. Her blonde hair was swept back from her face and secured with a lavender silk bow. Gold hoops glimmered in her earlobes.

She leaned closer to the mirror, checking her makeup. A light coat of foundation accented her ivory skin tones, and pale peach blush and peach gloss provided some color. She added an extra coat of mascara and curled her eyelashes. She knelt down, tying a double knot in her shoelaces so she wouldn't trip if they did any hiking.

Even though the temperature was expected to climb to the eighties and the sun was shining, there was a pleasant breeze rippling the oaks beyond her window.

The sound of a car pulling into her driveway brought her quickly to her feet. Grabbing her leather shoulder bag from the dresser, she hurried to unlock the front door.

At the sight of Matt, dressed in boots, jeans, and a sky blue polo—which deepened the blue of his eyes—her heart gave a crazy little flutter.

"Good morning," he said pleasantly.

"Good morning," she smiled. "Look, I want to show you something."

He stepped inside the living room, and she pointed toward the lush green fern that graced her window.

"How did you know it was exactly what I needed there?"

He grinned and shrugged. "I didn't."

"And Granny is so pleased! Matt, that was such a nice thing to do."

"You and your grandmother are very nice people." Their eyes held for a few seconds before he took a deep breath and glanced around the living room.

"Do you own this?" he asked.

"No, I'm just renting. My mother remarried while I was in school. When I moved back here to teach, I thought I should give the newlyweds their privacy." She smiled as she dropped her house key into her shoulder bag, then tucked the strap over her shoulder. "They're on vacation in Maine this summer."

"Do you like your stepfather?"

Laurel closed the door, checked to be sure it was locked then glanced at Matt. "I prefer to think of Hal as a friend."

His hand slipped casually around her elbow as they crossed the yard to his vehicle.

"I don't mean to sound as though I don't like Hal. I do," she explained. "It's just that I've known him all my life—he owned the hardware store until he retired. But he can't replace my father, and I have a silly hang-up about even calling him a stepfather. Maybe I'll conquer that."

"You must have been very close to your dad," he said, opening the car door for her.

"I was. But I do like Hal. I think he's been good for Mom, and she certainly deserves to be happy. She's a great lady."

"I'm sure she is. She has a great daughter," he grinned, closing the door.

As he came around the front of the car, Laurel's eyes traced the features of his face—high forehead, distinctive brow line, nice cheekbones, aquiline nose, firm mouth. She bit her lip and looked back toward the house. Did every woman consider him as handsome as she did? She'd always believed in looking beyond the physical attributes of a person. Why was she falling for a man so gorgeous?

Falling! She snapped her eyes shut, trying to correct herself. He was simply a friend; that was all.

He opened the car door, and slid in under the wheel.

"I've looked forward to this day all week long," he said, cranking the engine and pressing a boot to the accelerator.

"You'll find the arts community very interesting," she replied, as he backed out of the drive and drove down Elm Street.

"I'm sure I will. But I was also looking forward to spending the day with you."

She smiled at him, then looked out the window.

"Better slow down when you pass Fat's place. Sometimes those men get detained in the middle of the street, swapping fishing stories."

"Fats?" he repeated incredulously.

"He owns the service station on the corner," Laurel laughed, waving to three men seated on a bench near the door, whittling and swapping tales. "You see the guy sitting in the middle, wearing a fireman's hat? That's Billy. He's in his forties, but he's our 'boy.' He's simple-minded, but everyone humors him. He thinks he runs the town."

Matt's eyes widened on Billy before returning to Laurel. "Are you serious?"

"Sure. And keep an eye out for Ol' Major when you turn the corner."

"Who?"

"A bluetick hound that wandered down from the parkway and took up residence. He lives in the park, but about this time every day he drags himself across the street to the grocery. Jim, in the meat department, will give him a bone."

Matt threw back his head and laughed. "Laurel, I know you're putting me on."

"I'm not!" she exclaimed, then laughed too as the worries of the past week were suddenly forgotten. "You see, this is why I love living here. There's no place like it."

"What makes it so special? For you, I mean?"

"I told you before, it's guarded by the angels," she replied seriously.

"Yeah, sure." His eyes teased her.

She smiled. "There's a story told by the old timers about the first wagon train that came through. The wagons stopped because there was some illness among the people. They made camp, expecting to bury some of the people in the valley the next day.

"But just after sunrise, when they were building their morning fires, someone looked up in the sky and saw a cloud shaped like an angel. The entire camp was alerted; one woman brought out a book with a picture of an angel. Everyone agreed the shape of the clouds resembled an angel. 'We'll be all right,' the woman said. 'An angel is watching over us.' And, remarkably, all the people got well. The people decided to make their homes here permanently. Of course, they called the place Angel Valley."

"That's quite a story," Matt said. "How accurate is it, do you suppose?"

Laurel shrugged. "I don't really know. But people here do seem happier and more content."

Matt nodded. "Half of America would like to spend a few days here and unwind."

"Well," Laurel sighed, "I hope half of America will stay over in the tourist areas and leave our sleepy little community to itself. We like things just the way they are."

"I won't argue with that, even though I make a living adding shopping centers and new buildings where they're needed."

"Doesn't it bother you to do that?" she asked.

He looked at her. "Bother me? No. If we put in a shopping center someplace, I figure we've helped the locals as well."

"But you destroy...something," she fumbled for the right way to express herself.

"Please! I have to deal with environmentalists and do-gooders every day. When I'm up here, I want to forget it."

Laurel felt her temper rising. "Perhaps those *do-gooders* have a point."

His blue eyes darkened as he looked across at her. She bit her lip. They hadn't gone a mile, and she'd already made him angry. She turned and stared straight ahead. There was no point in pursuing this conversation; she could see they were poles apart in their views.

"Don't worry, I won't do any developing here."

"Good," she replied in a calmer voice. They both were making a concession, and it was time to think of something else. She didn't want to ruin the day.

Matt pushed a tape into the deck, a soft instrumental that filled the summer morning and prompted a mood of relaxation as they made their way toward Gatlinburg.

Laurel pressed her head back against the soft seat, allowing the soothing music to flow over her. Her taut nerves relaxed, and she took a long deep breath. From the corner of her eye, she stole a glimpse at Matt.

He, too, had become silent, smoothly guiding the wheel, occasionally glancing right and left at the lush mountain valleys bordering the highway. Once or twice he leaned forward on the wheel, peering upward at the towering mountains. An easy compatible silence enclosed them, and Laurel found herself surprised at the way her nervousness had given way to contentment as they drove toward Gatlinburg.

Eight

❧

"Thank you," he said, after a while.

She rolled her head on the seat and squinted at him. "For what?" she asked, lifting an eyebrow.

"For not feeling that you have to drown every silence with words. So many people try to keep a conversation going when it isn't necessary."

She returned his smile. "Sometimes it's best to let nature do the talking."

He chuckled. "Yep, you're right."

She merely shrugged and smiled. *Here*, she thought, *is the perfect place for silence.* She didn't want to think about the other women he had dated nor go any further with his impressions of her.

"How was your week?" he asked casually.

"Good," she replied, keeping her tone light and easy. "And yours?"

"Busy as always, but I don't mind. I seem to be turning into a workaholic, and I don't want to do that; but the truth is, I'm surprised at how much I enjoy the family business."

"That's great," Laurel replied.

"What I don't like is living in Atlanta. That was one of the reasons I was so agreeable to being sent off to boarding school. Dad told me my weekends would be spent on outings around Lookout Mountain." He glanced at her. "You're lucky to have grown up here in the Smokies. Mountains seem to do good things for the soul."

Laurel nodded thoughtfully. "I agree."

Matt sighed. "One of the ironies of all the freedom we have today is that we have no choice over where we're born. Or to whom."

She glanced at him as she pondered those words. Had he planned to make that point to emphasize that he couldn't help being Madeline's son, inheriting the advantages and disadvantages of being a Wentworth? Or had the statement simply slipped out in conversation?

"You're right," she conceded. He had a point, and that prompted her to consider their relationship in a different way.

He slowed the Jeep at the outskirts of Gatlinburg. The little hamlet was a beehive of activity, with the streets jammed with cars and motor homes bearing license plates from practically every state in the union.

"Is this typical for summer?" Matt asked, trying to negotiate the Jeep between a luxurious motor home and a farm truck, parked along the narrow street.

"Sometimes it's much worse. Over 10 million people come through the Smokies every year."

"Ten million?" Matt gasped. "You gotta be kidding!"

"Nope. Many come around holidays, like the Fourth of July, or in October when the leaves are in color. During the Christmas season, there are parades, Yule-log burnings, and a festival of lights. It's absolutely wonderful."

"But with all those people...," he shook his head doubtfully.

"Strangely enough, folks are polite to one another. It must have something to do with their being on vacation and feeling happier and more relaxed."

Finally, after wedging past quaint shops and restaurants lined with cars, they were on the highway that led north, and within a few minutes reached the brown sign marking the turn-off to the arts and crafts community. Once there, traffic was no longer a problem as more shops and cottages of the Glades came into view.

"The city's law requires the craftspeople to sell handmade items, so the logos you see on the outside of these places means the items within are authentic, made by the people who live here."

"That's interesting. Where do we start?"

"Want to just park the car and walk? That way we can take our time."

They took their time, for sure, strolling over front porches where all manner of crafts were displayed. The people lived in cabins or small cottages that had been expanded to house the family and their wares. As they made their way from one cottage to another, shopping fever took hold, and both Matt and Laurel purchased armloads of items. Several hours later, exhausted and happy, they called it quits. Laurel had a new broom, some pottery, and an assortment of sweetly scented candles, all sizes and shapes.

Matt had been forced to return for the car, popping the tailgate down in order to load all of his purchases into the rear. Laurel couldn't believe the little-boy excitement that gripped him, putting a sparkle in his blue eyes, and bringing quick and easy laughter to his lips. He'd purchased everything from art to woodwork.

When they finally collapsed in the front seat of the car, Laurel turned to assess the huge pile in the rear of the Jeep. "What are you going to do with all this?"

"Some of it will go back to Atlanta for the office and for my house, and I'll leave a few pieces here."

He turned and looked at her. His hair was slightly tousled, with a strand drooping over his forehead; his blue eyes glowed, and there was a dribble of molasses on his shirt from the sorghum they had sampled.

"You did have a good time, didn't you?" she said, digging a Kleenex tissue out of her purse and dabbing at the stain on his shirt.

He captured her hand, lifting her fingers to his lips. "The best time ever."

"Ever? I don't believe you."

"I'm really a simple guy at heart. I believe that old adage about the best things in life being free."

Laurel turned and pointed to the back of the Jeep where the items they had bought were heaped in piles. "None of that was free."

"No, but people's smiles and laughter are free. And genuine friendship doesn't have a price."

Their eyes locked as his lips brushed her fingers again and her heart began to hammer. She recalled how Granny had been favorably impressed with Matt, and Laurel believed he really was a good person. Suddenly, it didn't matter to her about his mother or his sister; all that mattered was that she, too, was having more fun than she'd had in her whole life. Laurel was not going to examine all the reasons or ponder what was building in her heart. She was simply going to enjoy herself.

She folded her hands in her lap, absently caressing the fingers he had kissed.

"Tell me about yourself," he said, starting the engine and steering the car back onto the narrow road.

"Well," she crossed her arms and mentally scanned the years, trying to summarize what was important. "I've told you about my life," she replied. "I was born and raised in Angel Valley, went away to college, taught a year in Marietta, came home, and went to work at my old alma mater."

"Those are facts," he said, grinning at her. "I was hoping for the small details like...have you ever been in love?"

She hesitated. "I once imagined I was. As it turned out, he was not the guy I thought he was."

"What attracted you to him?"

Laurel shrugged. "He had a charming personality, but I couldn't trust him. Or believe him, for that matter. I suppose his character was shaped by an unstable home life—his mother was married and divorced several times. Maybe that had something to do with his inability to play fair in a relationship. The word *commitment* was not in his vocabulary."

Matt nodded. "I've known people like that."

His grip tightened on the steering wheel as he passed a huge motor home, inching along the highway. "To be perfectly honest, I've been pretty leery of women. If your theory of home life is true, maybe my reaction to women has been shaped by my mother who is, shall we say, a woman of moods. As for commitment, I've never stayed with one person for long either. That isn't because I'm afraid of commitment; I think it's because I don't want to be dishonest with someone."

Laurel listened carefully, amazed that he was being so frank with her, discussing something so personal.

"I've always believed you have to really like a person in order to love them," he continued. "Sometimes I worry that maybe I spend too much time looking for the flaws in a person. It's just that...so many people aren't what they seem. I don't want to make a mistake."

"Yes, but everyone has flaws."

He grinned. "I know. And I'm painfully aware of my own. As for commitment, Dad set a good example for me. Mother can be difficult, as you've experienced firsthand. Yet Dad loved her, and as far as I know, they were always faithful to one another. When he died, she was brokenhearted."

Laurel nodded, thinking perhaps she should try to be more tolerant of the woman.

He glanced from the road to Laurel. "How did your mother handle it when your father died?"

Laurel pressed her head against the seat, studying the mountains towering above them. "She was brokenhearted, too. She cried a lot, and she prayed a lot."

"Maybe that's the difference. My mother is not a religious person. She's very bitter about it, in fact. I'd never been to church until I went to live with my grandmother. I became a Christian during that time, and in doing so, a whole new world opened to me."

Laurel turned and smiled at him. "Almost from the beginning, I knew you were different from...," she bit her lip.

"From Mother and Anna Lee. Maybe you can help Anna Lee; I'm afraid it's too late to do much with Mother."

"It's never too late." She wondered if she should tell him about Monday. Finally, she decided she had no choice. He would probably hear about it from Madeline; so why not tell him her side of the story?

Laurel took a deep breath. "Matt, I have to tell you something. On Monday, Anna Lee and I went to the library and then stopped by the church to avoid a rainstorm." She turned to him, unaware how much her blue eyes reflected the hurt Madeline had inflicted. "Anna Lee enjoyed a children's program at the church, but your mother was upset that we went."

He shook his head, frowning. "I'm sorry, Laurel. Sometimes Mother is a real pain. Do what you can for Anna Lee, and just try to tolerate Mother."

"Everything will work out," she said, and suddenly she meant it. Sharing her concern had relieved her frustrations. She took a deep breath, feeling better about the coming week where her work was concerned. Then she recalled that Matt had already had one talk with his mother about her; another one could mean the end of her summer job, which she still wanted to keep, in spite of everything that had happened.

"I would appreciate it if you wouldn't mention this conversation to her," Laurel said. "I'm trying to handle things myself."

"I know you are. And I respect you for it. People think because I've inherited the company and the privileges of the Wentworths, that my life is easy and my mother listens to me. It never has been that way."

The rest of the journey passed pleasantly, and darkness was settling over the countryside by the time they returned to Angel Valley.

"Where do you suggest we go for dinner?" he asked, as the scattered lights of town greeted them.

She dreaded the news she must break, for it ruined any plans for their evening together. Finally, she hit on an alternative.

"My place," she said with a smile. "I'm afraid I had obligated myself to the Mountaineers before you called."

"The Mountaineers?" Over the muted lights of the dashboard, his expression was one of total disbelief.

"The Music Mountaineers. I belong to a little group of musicians who play for special events. I had forgotten until after you called that I promised to practice with them this evening for an event coming up soon."

He was quiet for a moment, and she sensed his disappointment. "Isn't there any way you can cancel? Or reschedule?"

"I'm afraid not. We had to cancel last week because of the fair. This is the last time we'll get together before Jessica's wedding."

"Are you playing at the wedding?" he asked, slightly less incredulous, yet disbelief still dominated his tone.

"At the reception. She's having a variety of music. She wanted some music that reflected her upbringing. She's marrying a guy from Boston, and this way of life is new to his family."

"I'll bet." The answer held a note of sarcasm as he pulled into her driveway. "Then I won't keep you," he said.

"Matt," she reached forward to touch his hand, "please don't be upset. I've had a wonderful day. If I hadn't already committed myself, you know I'd love having dinner with you. I could prepare a...," her mind sped through the choices in her cabinet, "a hot dog for you."

"A hot dog," he repeated, squinting through the darkness to see her. "You know, you have a way of calming me when I'd normally be irritated. I guess it's because it's difficult to stay mad at you. You're such a nice person."

"Oh, you're just saying that because I mentioned food," she teased. "And don't you just love a hot dog, smothered with mustard and ketchup and sliced onions? And maybe a sweet pickle chopped up on top?"

He burst into laughter. "No, I don't just love it." He squeezed her hand. "But I love being with you. So...yes. I'll take a hot dog."

They laughed as they spilled out of the Jeep and groped their way through the darkness to the front porch.

"I should have a left a light on," she said, plundering through her purse in search of the house key. Finally, when her fingers had closed around it and she was about to insert the key in the lock, she felt Matt's arm around her shoulders.

Gently, he pulled her against his chest. With the soft night breeze slipping over them, and the distant smell of flowers in bloom, his lips brushed hers in a feather-light caress. It was a sweet moment, capping off the wonderful day they had shared.

Then suddenly the house key dropped from Laurel's hand, clanging loudly against the concrete porch. Both were down on hands and knees, scrambling around the flower pots, when a vehicle pulled in front of the house and a horn blared.

Laurel jumped up, key in hand, and squinted toward the car.

"Laurel, you up there?"

Jim Willingham's unmistakable voice floated through the darkness.

"We just got home," she called. "I'm unlocking the door. Want to come in?" *I can't just leave Jim and Rosemary sitting out in the darkness.* "Sorry, but I have no choice," she muttered under her breath to Matthew.

The slam of doors answered her invitation, and she quickly turned the key in the lock, pushed the door open, and groped for the light switch inside.

The front porch came to life beneath the small bulb overhead, encircling Matt and Laurel in a small wreath of gold. Jim and Rosemary, arms linked in an effort to keep from stumbling in the darkness, were clearly surprised. They stopped and exchanged quick glances with one another.

"We're just getting back from Gatlinburg," Laurel explained.

The couple smiled vacantly, still frozen in their path, obviously torn between coming inside and turning back to the car.

Jim cleared his throat. "You said the G string on your dulcimer needed tuning. We thought we'd come by before practice so I could check it out."

Laurel remembered. "That's right, and I'm glad you stopped by. Please—come on in."

Hesitantly, the couple approached the porch and Matt stepped forward, his hand extended.

"I'm Matt Wentworth," he said politely.

"Jim Willingham." They shook hands. "And this is my wife, Rosemary."

"Nice to meet you," Matt said. "Maybe I should let you guys get on with your plans."

"Matt, come on in," Laurel insisted. "We can still have that hot dog. Jim, Rosemary, have you eaten?"

Rosemary, an attractive blonde who was Laurel's best friend, smiled shyly. "We ate earlier, thank you. Laurel, we'll come back later."

"Don't be silly. Come to think of it, you've arrived at the perfect time." Her eyes twinkled as she looked at Matt.

Her humor was lost on Jim and Rosemary; Matt, however, caught the joke and grinned as everyone entered the kitchen and settled around the kitchen table. Matt and Jim discussed weather and politics while Rosemary helped Laurel prepare the food. Soon, Laurel and Matt were devouring "dressed dogs," as Laurel laughingly called them, and huge glasses of iced tea.

"Have you talked with Jessica?" Rosemary asked.

"Not since last week. She told me that she and her fiancé aren't coming until the day before the wedding. There won't be time for us to give her a party."

Rosemary sighed. "I know, but I'm just glad the wedding is here."

Laurel turned to Matt. "Rosemary, Jessica, and I were best friends in high school. Jessica's father worked for a pharmaceutical company in Knoxville and commuted so the family could live in Angel Valley. When we graduated from high school, his company transferred him to Louisville."

"But your friend is coming here to get married?" Matt asked.

Laurel nodded. "It'll be a small wedding, but she insisted on having Rosemary and me for her bridesmaids."

"And we're helping with the music, as well," Rosemary grinned, glancing at Jim who was testing the strings on Laurel's dulcimer. With his ear tilted while he strummed, his eyes wandered idly over the kitchen. Suddenly he began to chuckle.

"What's wrong with you?" Rosemary smiled.

"You and Laurel and your buckeyes!" He indicated the shelf beside the table. Along with her books, Laurel had displayed a buckeye in the crystal pickle dish she had inherited from her great-grandmother.

"Sure!" Rosemary responded. "Buckeyes are important to a mountain woman."

Sheepishly, Laurel glanced at Matt, who was clearly puzzled.

"Matt, we're all a little bit crazy," Laurel said. "In case you haven't already figured that out."

Matt's eyes wandered from Rosemary to Jim to the buckeye and back to Laurel. "No, but what's with the buckeye?"

Jim stopped strumming and grinned at Matt. "Women consider buckeyes a symbol of love."

Matt looked back at the buckeye, obviously trying to figure it out on his own.

Rosemary spoke up first. "There are two seeds inside a buckeye, and they fit together in one pod. It's an old mountain tradition here for couples planning to be married to open the husk. The man and woman each take a seed."

She looked across at Jim and smiled with eyes full of love. "We had our seeds with us at the wedding. When the preacher read the passage from the Bible where two become one...," her voice trailed as her eyes moved from Laurel to Matt. "I guess you think we're pretty silly."

"Not at all," Matt replied. "Sounds like a nice tradition." He glanced back at Laurel. "So have you opened your buckeye?"

113

She saw that a grin was forming on his lips now, and she laughed at the question. "Nope. Mom and Dad kept buckeyes in their kitchen and gave one to me. It's purely sentimental," she said, and everyone looked at the little buckeye in the crystal dish. "I just hope that someday I can have the kind of marriage my parents had."

Laurel spoke out of love and good memories, and she was unaware for a moment of the silence that followed. When she looked back at the group seated at the kitchen table, Jim and Rosemary were holding hands, smiling into each other's eyes, while Matt was staring at her. Then suddenly he stood up, glancing at the kitchen phone.

"Laurel, I need to check with my answering service," he said. "Do you mind if I use your phone?"

"Go right ahead." She dashed over to clear the clutter from the kitchen counter. As he reached for the phone, she grabbed the notepad and pen she kept nearby and handed it to him. "Well, is that dulcimer going to do its job?" she asked Jim, as she returned to the table and took a seat.

"Hope so," Jim answered, checking the string again.

Laurel glanced at Rosemary who gave her a thumbs-up sign, and suddenly they were on the brink of lapsing into their school-girl giggles.

Jim shook his head, looking from one woman to the other. He had grown accustomed to their antics.

Matt jotted something on the pad, and began to dial another number.

"I hope Blake's folks aren't too stuffy," Rosemary said, trying to steer the subject in a different direction. "What if someone starts clogging at the reception?"

Laurel laughed. "If they want mountain music, the clogging goes with it!"

Matt came back to the table with a smile on his face. "We've had an offer on one of our shopping centers." His eyes gleamed as he looked at Laurel, then the dulcimer. "Maybe I'll accept that offer and use the money to build a plant here for making dulcimers," he teased.

"No plants, thank you!" Laurel answered quickly.

"Well," he said, more seriously, "the bad news is that I have to drive back to Atlanta tonight to go over the offer. They're wanting to close on this right away."

"Oh, too bad." Laurel said, unable to keep the disappointment from her voice. "Not about the sale, but about your having to make that long drive tonight."

He shrugged. "I need to call a meeting with my people first thing in the morning."

Jim and Rosemary exchanged glances and came quickly to their feet. "We're going on over to unlock the church, Laurel. Take your time."

Jim turned to Matt. "Nice meeting you. Why don't you come to Jessica's wedding and hear our music?"

Matt looked from the Willinghams back to Laurel. "Maybe I will."

"See you later," Laurel called to the couple as they slipped out of the house. She turned to Matt. "Come if you want to, but don't feel like..."

He reached forward to cup her chin. "If it's a chance to be with you, I want to." He stared down into her eyes for several seconds, while Laurel's heart raced. Then he bent down and kissed her gently. "Wish I didn't have to leave," he said wistfully.

She nodded. "I know. Drive carefully."

He sighed. "I will. Thanks for a special day." He hesitated at the door, looking back at her.

"It was special for me, too," she said, as their eyes held for a moment.

He winked at her then walked through the door, closing it softly behind him.

Laurel watched him go, savoring the moment, listening to the sound of his Jeep fading into the night. He was gone and already she missed being with him. What a wonderful day it had been!

As she closed the door, her eyes drifted to the beautiful green fern in the hanging basket. She wandered to the window, gently touching the fern and smiling to herself. She was glad she had a reminder of Matt, although she didn't seem to need one.

She looked out into the darkness, lifting her eyes to the star-filled sky. She hadn't wished on a star in years, but tonight she felt inclined to make a wish—one that concerned Matt Wentworth.

Nine

Another week stretched before Laurel, one she tried to plan carefully as she drove toward Raven Ridge. The weatherman had predicted beautiful weather for the day and the next, but then rain was suppose to move in on Wednesday.

She had called the Wentworth house last night, dreading a conversation with Madeline. To her relief, Anna Lee had answered the phone. Laurel explained her reasons for planning their field trip for Monday or Tuesday, asking Anna Lee to check with her mother. Anna Lee had called right back, saying they could go on Monday. Her voice betrayed her excitement as she asked Laurel how to dress.

"Jeans and a comfortable top. Maybe you better throw in a heavy sweater or windbreaker. Do you have any hiking boots?

"No," Anna Lee groaned.

"Then tennis shoes will be fine. We'll have a good time, Anna Lee," she had added, hoping the mention of hiking boots hadn't scared her off.

"I hope so..."

꧁

Now, as Laurel turned up the driveway, glancing down at her own jeans, sweatshirt, and hiking boots, she wondered if Mrs. Wentworth would find fault with her clothes. She seemed to search for anything to criticize.

Her little car groaned and sputtered up the incline, reminding her she was overdue on getting the convertible serviced. Finally, at the top of the hill, the car gained momentum and came to life in a spurt, scattering gravel in all directions and announcing her arrival.

A curtain fluttered on the second floor. A quick glance confirmed Madeline's disapproving scowl. Laurel gave her a wide smile, almost out of spite, then cut the engine, glancing around the car seat. She decided to leave her purse and books, since she wanted to leave right away.

She hopped out and hurried up the walk, reaching up to secure the clasp on her ponytail. She had not worn makeup for their field trip. No doubt, Madeline would size her up as every inch the mountaineer, but she no longer cared. She and Anna Lee were going to have a good time, in spite of Madeline and her moods.

Anna Lee was standing in the doorway, a sweater thrown over her arm. She carried a small camera, which Laurel took as a good indication that Anna Lee was going to try to enjoy herself.

"Ready?" Laurel smiled, as her eyes ran down Anna Lee's fancy denim shirt and another tight pair of designer jeans. She wore tennis shoes, which looked sturdy, although the laces were trailing. "Before we leave, you'd better tie a double knot in your shoe laces."

Surprised, Anna Lee looked from Laurel to her feet and

leaned down to follow the suggestion. In the background, Laurel heard a muffled cough, and she suspected Madeline was hovering somewhere, listening. If so, she'd learn that Laurel had some common sense when it came to taking care of her students, despite her resentment over the stopoff at the church and their fun with Clarence the Clown.

"I see you brought your camera," Laurel commented as they walked to the car.

Anna Lee glanced at her. "I like to take pictures," she muttered.

"Good! You should get some good ones today. Maybe you can give me a lesson; I've always had a problem with my pictures; they tend to be lopsided!"

Anna Lee turned quickly, her eyes lighting for a moment. "You have to center your subject."

Laurel nodded as they got in the car. "I get impatient, afraid someone will make a move before I can snap the picture. Have you had any courses in photography?" Laurel asked, starting the car.

"In summer camp one year." She laid down her sweater on the front seat, carefully placing the camera on top. Then she turned to Laurel. "Will there be any more of those circuses?" Anna Lee asked, out of Madeline's earshot.

Laurel glanced at her. "There might be one later on in Maryville. Our pastor's sister is youth director at a church over there. Sometimes Tammy—that's the sister—likes to have people from our church come over for a program. And sometimes her youth group comes here."

"Is Maryville too far for us to go? If they have a program, I mean."

Laurel peered over the steering wheel to the road, trying to drive more cautiously with Anna Lee in the car. "No, it isn't too far, but I don't know what your mother would say about our going."

Anna Lee sighed heavily, slumping lower in the seat. "Sometimes I hate her," she said quietly. "She'll come into my room and nag me about trying to be thin or smart or witty. I've never been able to please her."

Laurel stared, startled by her statement. She searched her mind for an appropriate remark but could think of nothing. Then she recalled something she and Anna Lee had heard at Bible school: *God gives folks the right words at the right time!*

"Remember what Clarence the Clown told the boys and girls? They shouldn't hold grudges, that grudges make us sick inside." It always amazed Laurel how Billy, as Clarence the Clown, could deliver simple truths that held perfect logic.

"Try to be more tolerant of your mother," Laurel spoke gently. "She's been through a difficult time, and I know you have as well. But, you see, your life is just beginning, really. You'll grow up and do all kinds of interesting things. Maybe you'll be a professional photographer some day. On the contrary, your mother may feel as mine did—that her life is passing by, and she'll grow old alone."

Anna Lee made no response, but Laurel thought her features seemed to relax a bit, and the scowl slowly disappeared from her face. Because she was desperate to make Anna Lee feel better, Laurel realized she might be making a rash promise, but she couldn't help herself as she spoke up.

"I'll let you know if I hear of a program some place that sounds like fun; maybe we can relate it to school work."

"Thanks, Laurel!" Anna Lee smiled.

The dull, lifeless gaze that had met Laurel when they were first introduced had been transformed into a wistful expression over the past weeks, and now Laurel's spirits lifted as well.

"You're welcome," she answered. "I like to do things together."

"You're just saying that; you don't really mean it!"

Fortunately, Laurel had reached the main highway and had stopped for traffic; otherwise, she might have stomped the accelerator instead of the brake. She was shocked almost speechless by Anna Lee's abrupt change. She took a deep breath, choosing her words as she turned to the girl. Tiny red blotches dotted each of her cheeks.

"Of course I mean it." Laurel spoke in a clear, firm voice. "I never say anything I don't mean, and I don't appreciate you suggesting that I would."

She wasn't really angry, but she wanted to drive the point home so that Anna Lee wouldn't have any doubts that Laurel wanted to spend time with her.

Anna Lee's eyebrows peaked as she looked at Laurel and saw the stern reproach in her eyes.

"I just wanted to be sure," she said vaguely, turning to stare out the window.

"Well, you can be sure."

She reached forward and inserted an Amy Grant tape into the tape deck.

"Do you like my brother?" Anna Lee asked.

Laurel caught her breath. Honestly, this girl kept her on her toes every minute.

121

"He seems nice," Laurel said, hoping to sidetrack the issue.

"He has lots of girlfriends in Atlanta, but I don't like any of them."

Laurel tried not to think about all the other girls. She had to keep her mind on her driving.

When Anna Lee realized she wasn't going to get any response from Laurel, she tried another tack.

"I heard what Mother said, and you did too, didn't you?"

"Said about what?" she asked, playing dumb, although she knew what was coming.

"About you being a mountaineer."

Laurel glanced at Anna Lee. She wasn't going to lie to her.

"Yes, I did."

"How did it make you feel?"

Laurel pressed her tense shoulders against the back of the seat, wishing she could have avoided this. "How would it make you feel?"

"Terrible. Mother makes everyone feel terrible."

Luckily, they had reached the parkway, and as Laurel turned up the ramp, she leaned forward and peered through her windshield to the mountain range in the distance.

"Well, Anna Lee, I suppose this would be a good time for a geography lesson, how about it?"

"You're just trying to change the subject."

"Yep, I'd like to change the subject. But it's also time for a geography lesson, so put on your thinking cap."

Anna Lee looked surprised. "Here? How?"

"Take a look at that towering mountain range out there—the

122

Great Smoky Mountains. They're a part of the Appalachian Mountain Range that stretches down into your state, as well. Know why these mountains are called the Smokies?"

"Because of that bluish haze that hangs over them."

"Right. You can find some haze on mountains in other places, but there's more haze here because we get lots more rain—fifty to sixty inches a year—and have more trees. And the reason for the haze is the millions of shrubs and trees that give off hydrocarbon—"

"*What?*"

"Vapor and oil. These form little drops that stick to the mountain peaks. Now here's your history lesson. Remember we're studying about the Trail of Tears? Well, the Cherokees once owned these valleys and mountains. They called the mountains *Shagonigei,* which means 'blue smoke.' Some of the Indians here went on the Trail of Tears."

Anna Lee suddenly looked bleak. "That's sad."

"It's very sad." Laurel sighed as she guided her car into a rest stop where she felt they would be safe. She could lock the car, and she knew the best trails to hike from that location.

She glanced across at Anna Lee, who had slumped into her seat.

"Now what is it?" Laurel asking, acknowledging the change.

"I wish I could stay in Angel Valley and never go back to Atlanta. I hate it there!"

Again, bitterness edged her words, and Laurel could see the child was overflowing with anger and hostility.

"Anna Lee," she paused, taking a deep breath, "we all have to do things we don't want to do, but—"

"What do you hate to do?" Anna Lee cut in.

Laurel considered the question for several seconds, and realized, guiltily, that she lived her life pretty much as it suited her. She knew she was remarkably lucky, and searched her heart for something that honestly bothered her.

"I hate to deal with difficult situations," she finally admitted. "And frankly, Anna Lee, this job has been difficult at times. But I'm glad I took it. You're making progress, you know, and that makes me happy. So you see, we just have to take the bitter with the sweet."

Anna Lee thought that over as Laurel reached into the back seat for their windbreakers.

"I don't want to walk a lot," Anna Lee protested, accepting her jacket.

"This is an easy trail; you shouldn't have a problem. Believe me, I've given our little trip a lot of thought."

"Why?" Anna Lee asked, unbuckling her seat belt and reaching for her camera.

"Because I want you to enjoy it."

Anna Lee looked into Laurel's hazel eyes for a moment. Then, satisfied that Laurel meant what she had said, she nodded. "Thanks."

Laurel grabbed a small paperback with pictures and descriptions of plants and trees. Stuffing it into the pocket of her jacket as they got out, she locked the car and they set off toward the trail. Laurel reminded herself to slow her usual pace to make allowances for Anna Lee's weight.

"Find that one, and tell me when you do," she instructed, pointing to the sweet gum as she handed Anna Lee the book.

Anna Lee frowned, turning pages. Yet when she came upon the tree, she looked pleased.

As they progressed along the trail, Anna Lee identified the yellow poplar, along with the spruce and fir and hemlock. Here and there, she stopped to take pictures, but Laurel didn't mind. She wanted Anna Lee to have a good time.

"See that one?" Laurel pointed. "A white flower blooms on it in the spring. Guess what the flower is called?"

Anna Lee consulted the book again. "I can't find it."

"I'll tell you. The flower is a laurel. It's my namesake," she smiled as Anna Lee lifted her camera and snapped a picture before they trudged on. "My father was a forest ranger. He loved the woods. When I was born, he told Mom I was as pretty as a mountain laurel in the spring." She tweaked her nose. "I'll bet I was just a wrinkled little baby with a red face, don't you?"

Anna Lee looked at her solemnly. "No. You were probably always pretty and...thin."

"I don't know about the pretty part, but I haven't always been thin. I just decided in high school that I'd better eat right and get exercise. I felt it was important," she said, hoping she could make a point without offending Anna Lee.

"There's a funny story about my name," she said, smoothly switching the subject. "My best friends in school were Rosemary Watts and Jessica Thorne. We went everywhere together; once we went to a school dance without dates and the guys said, 'Well, here come the wallflowers: a laurel and a rose with a thorn.'"

Anna Lee laughed softly, listening to Laurel's words.

"And after that, everyone called us the wallflowers! It was so humiliating. Whew, let's sit down," Laurel said, pressing a hand to her chest. "My breath is getting short. I have to tell you, my friend, you have more stamina than I would have thought."

They found a dry spot beneath a hemlock and took a seat.

"When I'm taking pictures, I have more energy," Anna Lee said. She was panting but she didn't seem to realize it. Having a good time distracted her.

Laurel stared at her. "You know, Anna Lee, maybe you should pursue photography. It seems to bring you more pleasure than anything else. Have you spoken to your mother about it?"

She hesitated. "She knows. Dad...," her voice faltered, and she turned to look out across the valley, "bought me a camera when I went to camp, and he liked my pictures. We even had a dark room installed in the house...," her voice trailed, as she shifted and turned her face away from Laurel.

"You were very close to him, weren't you?" Laurel asked, staring at Anna Lee's back.

"Yes."

"I was close to my father, too," Laurel said. "After he died, I felt so alone, even though my mother was hurting, too. But somehow I could only think about my own pain." Her eyes moved over Anna Lee's stiff back. She seemed to want to avoid Laurel's eyes now, and Laurel wondered if she were crying.

"A Sunday school teacher gave me some special Bible verses that helped a lot, more than anything anyone had said to me, in fact. I read the verses every night when I went to bed and again in the morning when I awoke."

"What were the verses?" Anna Lee asked faintly.

Laurel opened her mouth to recite them, but then had a better idea.

126

"Would you like me to give you those verses? I still have them tucked away in my Bible, on the sheet of paper my teacher gave me. Since they were special to me, maybe they could help you."

"Don't you want to keep them?" she asked in a broken voice.

"I'd like you to have them. You see—" Laurel was looking at Anna Lee's back, but stopped talking as the girl's shoulders gave way to deep wrenching sobs. Laurel slipped to her knees before Anna Lee, moving around to where she could see her face, and when she did, her breath caught.

Thick tears poured down her cheeks. Her lips trembled, and her large body heaved as though someone were dealing her a mighty blow, one after another.

"I know it hurts, I know it hurts terribly," Laurel said gently, stretching her arms around Anna Lee. "But sometimes crying helps more than anything."

Anna Lee brokenly blurted something indistinguishable.

Laurel pulled her closer, trying to soothe her. "It gets better in time, Anna Lee. I know it's hard to believe that now, but trust me, it does get better."

Anna Lee pulled back from her, shaking her head. Her eyes were ravaged with pain, and she had sunk her teeth into her lower lip until it bled.

Laurel fumbled in her pocket for a Kleenex tissue and quickly dabbed at Anna Lee's lip.

"He's the only person who ever understood me," Anna Lee said, between gasps. "He knew I could never be all that Mother expects. He liked me the way I was, but..."

Satisfied the bleeding had stopped, Laurel returned the tissue to her pocket and rubbed Anna Lee's hand.

"But what, darling?"

Fresh tears filled her eyes and poured down her cheeks, as she spoke between gasps.

"But he always told me to be strong, that I had to be strong and not cry about things because Mother was so weak. She has terrible headaches and she gets sick and..."

"Oh, Anna Lee," Laurel exclaimed, hugging her tighter, "you've held everything inside, not wanting to make your mother sick, and you can't do that. Look what it's done to you!"

After speaking, Laurel was afraid Anna Lee might pull away from her. On the contrary, she relaxed in Laurel's arms, and even leaned against Laurel's shoulder as though the embrace felt good.

"From now on, I want you to cry when you feel like crying," Laurel said gently. "You can't bear everyone's burdens, just your own."

She said nothing more as Anna Lee slowly calmed down, and only the chirp of birds and the fluttering of little friends in the forest interrupted their silence.

After a long time, Anna Lee pulled back. She looked embarrassed as she rubbed the sweater over her face, wiping away her tears.

Laurel felt that she and Anna Lee had made a long journey to some dark haunted place and finally stumbled back to a safe place as the sun dropped a few rays around them.

"Anna Lee, you can talk to me anytime, about anything. It will be our own secret. I want you to feel that you can trust me. And you can cry with me anytime you want to. Agreed?"

Anna Lee nodded, wiping her eyes again.

"Hey," Laurel laughed suddenly, "we forgot all about

lunch." She glanced at her watch. "It's after one. You must be starved."

Anna Lee shook her head. "Not really."

"The picnic basket is in the back seat," Laurel said. "When we get back, we can have a sandwich. I brought a thermos of juice and two cups."

"Okay," Anna Lee answered. She didn't seem to mind a late lunch or the prospect of a mere sandwich.

Laurel smiled at her and reached out a hand. "Come on. I'm tired of being a teacher."

Shyly, Anna Lee took her hand. Arm in arm, they trudged back to the car.

Later, they drove home, singing to the radio and laughing. It was after 3:00 when Laurel pulled up before the huge house.

"Hope your mother wasn't worried," Laurel said, automatically glancing up at the window.

"I'll tell her I learned a lot," Anna Lee said, getting out of the car, her camera and sweater in hand. For the first time, a smile looked natural on her lips.

Laurel had just arrived home and was uncapping a bottle of apple juice when the telephone rang. She hesitated, wondering if Madeline was calling with a reprimand. For a moment she was tempted just to let it ring. Then she reminded herself there was no reason to fear a conversation with Madeline; she had nothing to hide. With that in mind, she answered in a strong voice.

"Hi."

It was Matt.

Laurel almost dropped the bottle of apple juice at the sound of his voice. A smile flew over her face as she gripped the phone tighter.

"Hi. How was that meeting?"

He groaned. "For two days I've been holed up in the conference room with lawyers. I'm getting cabin fever, which is why I'm calling. We've made some stipulations on that offer I told you about. The attorneys expect another week of haggling, and I've decided to let them earn their money. I'm taking some time off, and guess where I'd like to come?"

"Here," she said, smiling.

"Exactly. Are you free tomorrow afternoon?"

"Sure. The weather is supposed to be nice for another day or so. Want me to fix a picnic basket and think of some place to go?"

"Perfect. See you around the middle of the afternoon. If you've already left our house, I'll pick you up at your place."

She bit her lip. "Matt? Could we...would you mind just picking me up here? I'll need to return home first and..."

"And you don't want Mother's opinion on our plans?"

She laughed in spite of herself. "Yes."

"Point well taken. I'll be looking forward to the picnic."

"Me, too."

After they said goodbye and hung up, she hummed a romantic song she had heard on the way home. She couldn't believe how happy she felt over the prospect of seeing him again. She hurried to the refrigerator, already making plans for their picnic.

The next afternoon a picnic basket was packed and waiting with ham sandwiches, chips, potato salad, a thermos of tea, and a batch of chocolate-chip cookies. She had just finished dressing in jeans, a T-shirt, and Keds when she heard his car drive up.

She checked the mirror one more time. Her eyes sparkled, her cheeks held a natural blush, and the new conditioner she'd just applied to her hair brought out its golden shine.

As soon as Matt knocked on the door, Laurel grabbed the picnic basket from the kitchen table. She had planned a full afternoon and there was no time to waste.

She opened the door and smiled into his weary face.

"Hi. You look great," he said, as his eyes wandered down her slim frame.

"Hi. And you look tired," she said, touching his arm. "You did need a break, didn't you?"

His jeans and shirt were fresh, but his face held the shadow of a beard, and his eyes were haggard. He grinned. "I was exhausted, but I'm already feeling better." He relieved her of the picnic basket as they walked to his car and got in. "Where are we going? Not that I really care. Just to get back to the mountains and be with you is all that's important to me now."

Laurel smiled. "I thought it would be fun to take a drive through Cades Cove. Have you ever been there?"

"No, but I'm game."

"Game is why we're going! Cades Cove is a beautiful mountain valley with all kinds of wildlife protected by the park service. It was a frontier community until the park was established. The government bought up all the old farms and set the area aside to preserve it for history." She lifted a road map from the seat of the car and pointed to the highway they would follow as they drove off.

"You enjoy going there?"

"I love going there! And I think you will, too."

He grinned and shook his head. "A girl after my own heart."

Laurel shifted her eyes back to the houses along the road. He kept looking at her as though he were trying to read her thoughts. "I doubt that I'd have a chance at your heart, compared to all those sophisticated women in Atlanta."

He was silent for a moment. When he spoke, his answer startled her. "None of those women interest me as much as you do."

Her eyes flew back to him. He looked sincere as his eyes probed hers for a moment, as though he were waiting for a response. She turned to stare out the window, uncertain about what to say.

Matt cleared his throat. "Well, I see that the crowd has gathered." He was looking at the service station where several of the old timers were examining a fishing pole.

"Yep," she grinned. She was grateful for a change of subject.

"And should I watch out for the dog? Is it time for his afternoon bone?"

Laurel laughed harder. "No, he makes that trip in the morning."

Matt pounded his hand against the steering wheel in a playful manner. "How could I have forgotten?"

He, too, laughed now, and Laurel was relieved to see the lines of care disappear from his face.

"Do you expect that company to buy your shopping center?" she asked conversationally.

He was thoughtful for a moment as his Jeep left the little town and headed for the open road. "I think so. We may have to do some more haggling with the fine details, but...," he nodded his head as he glanced at her, "yes, I do. Then I'll have to worry about reinvesting the money."

"And that's a worry?" Laurel teased.

"Sometimes. Let's talk about your week."

"Gladly."

She told him about her field trip with Anna Lee, mentioning the educational aspects at first, then moving on to Anna Lee's interest in photography.

"Dad shared that interest with her," he said quietly, "and I'm glad. In some ways, he and Anna Lee were a lot alike."

"She told me that."

For a moment she was tempted to reveal the other things Anna Lee had said, but realized it would break a confidence, and that was unfair to Anna Lee when they finally were making some progress.

He slowed the Jeep as they approached the entrance to Cades Cove. "Well, here we are."

For once, Laurel was sorry to reach Cades Cove. She wanted Matt to go on talking, sharing personal things about his life. It was the only way she could really come to know who he was. But once they entered the narrow road within the park, his interest turned toward the lush green valley enclosed by the towering smoky peaks.

"This road goes one way," she warned him. "It makes an eleven-mile loop. At the next turn, look to the right meadow. Deer come out of the woods to graze there."

His eyes shot from the road to her and back as he leaned forward against the steering wheel, eagerly looking from right to left while watching the road.

Laurel smiled to herself. She had always believed that everyone still had a bit of the child within, and Matt confirmed it once again. She found it amazing how quickly he could slip from the role of "wealthy businessman" to "regular guy."

Her eyes slipped over his profile: once again admiring his looks. *I like him more than any man I've ever met. In fact...*

"Look, there's a deer over there, just like you promised." Matt pointed and then pulled over.

A car had stopped in front of them to take pictures, and Matt reached into the back seat for a pair of binoculars. "Here," he said, and handed the glasses to her. "You'll need to adjust the lens to suit your eyes."

"Thanks!" Laurel experimented until she had the doe in clear view. Just then, directly behind the doe, a baby deer stepped out of the woods.

"Matt, look!" She handed him the binoculars.

"Amazing," he said, watching the deer feed.

She was pleased that he seemed to enjoy nature as much as she did. The man was stealing her heart, and she seemed powerless to stop it from happening.

He lowered the binoculars and grinned, catching her eyes upon him.

"I'm glad you suggested this," he said, as he put the car in gear again. "Are these log structures the originals?" he asked, indicating the cabin they passed.

"Only one is an original. The others were moved in order to preserve them, but the ones we see are replicas of that first frontier community in 1820."

"Want to get out and explore?" Matt asked. "I've had a secret yen to build a log cabin."

"Then let's take a look. This might be more primitive than the one you have in mind!"

As they got out of the car and started up the path to the log cabin, Matt reached for her hand.

"I really enjoy being with you," he said, smiling as she turned to look up at him.

"Thanks. I like being with you, too."

It had turned into a wonderful afternoon for Laurel; she couldn't remember ever having more fun or enjoying being with anyone as much as Matt.

"I've always been fascinated with pioneer life," he said, turning to study the old log cabin. "I've read lots of books on the early settlers. It amazes me how much common sense they had. They could survive in the toughest conditions. I think most of us have turned into sissies compared to our forefathers."

"Life today is difficult in other ways," Laurel said, thinking of the conflicts she faced in her life and her work.

"Look at that," he said, hurrying on to inspect a notched corner on the end of the house. "That's real skill."

"The yellow poplar trees made good cabins," Laurel said. "Last year I started a project in my classroom that I expect to continue every year. We built a miniature log cabin. Harold Birdsong, who's a genius with wood, brings wood scraps over and shows us how to build it. It's a good chance for the kids to learn about pioneer life, as well. I schedule the project to be finished just before the Thanksgiving holiday, and on Wednesday we have a pilgrim's meal and give thanks for our new home."

He had turned his eyes from the cabin to look at her as she spoke. "You're amazing. I never had a teacher like you," he squeezed her hand. "It's probably a good thing. I wouldn't have been able to concentrate for looking at you. Of course, all the boys have a crush on you, right?"

She laughed. "No."

A family came out of the cabin, so Laurel and Matt moved on, clearing the path.

"In spring and fall, Old-Timers Day is held here. Families of the original settlers come back to fellowship and play their musical instruments—fiddles, dulcimers, juice harps. It's a lot of fun."

"Do you come? Did your family come as settlers?"

"No, but one of my students, Tommy Thompson, is a descendant. His parents invited me to come with them. We had a wonderful time."

They toured the cabin, inspecting every room, then wandered on out the back door. They walked for a while, ending up beneath a huge tree to survey a distant pasture where horses grazed.

"I can't imagine life in a simple setting like this," he said, staring at the landscape.

"It was a unique way of life. They farmed and harvested, using harvests as a social event during which they helped each other and had fun too." She paused, recalling what she had learned at Old-Timers Day. "That's when some heavy courting was done, too. Mrs. Thompson told me there was a custom in which a young man, finding an ear of red corn during husking, could kiss his girlfriend. That's how her great-great-grandparents got together."

Matt stared intently down at Laurel as she stopped to rest her back against a tree and look out over the pasture. He reached down to the ground, picking up an object.

"Look what I found," he said, his fist closed over something.

"What is it?"

"A kernel of red corn."

He leaned down and kissed her, then looked deeply into her eyes. For a moment, Laurel felt as though they were frozen in time. She was oblivious to everything beyond the handsome face above her, the blue eyes gleaming down into hers.

She swallowed, trying to recapture her senses. "Let me see that red corn," she said, averting her eyes to his hand.

He opened his palm. "What do you know? It's a little red rock. I must have been mistaken."

"Oh you!" she said, playfully swatting at his arm.

"Maybe if I look harder, I can find the real thing. Then I'll get another kiss," he said, winking at her.

A car had stopped nearby, from which two children spilled out, cameras in hand.

Matt sighed. "All good things must end. Speaking of good things, whatever you have in that basket is smelling better by the minute."

Laurel laughed. "I'm hungry, too. Why don't we head out of the park? I know a great picnic spot not far away."

He grinned. "You seem to have all the answers."

"Not all of them," she replied, and as he glanced briefly at her, she was certain he knew exactly what she meant.

They chose a picnic spot in a grassy meadow beside a chattering stream. Matt spread a blanket over the lush grass, and Laurel opened up the picnic basket. They dropped down on the soft cloth, relishing the food, and staring in awe at the breathtaking mountain view.

"I sometimes think about how this land must have looked to the first settlers who came here. Probably thought they'd found paradise," Matt said.

Laurel took a deep breath. "Yes, but I always feel sympathetic toward the Cherokee nation who fished the streams and hunted these beautiful meadows until we came along and rooted them out. Bullies, aren't we?"

Matt nodded. "Doesn't seem fair, does it?"

They ate in comfortable silence, with the gentle accompaniment of a crystal stream gurgling over stones.

"There's a waterfall not far from here," Laurel said. "When I was growing up, Dad would bring us here to picnic. I had planned for us to go there today, but I thought you might be too hungry to wait another twenty minutes."

"You thought right," Matt chuckled. "This spot is perfect, as far as I'm concerned. Did you picnic a lot growing up?" Matt asked, munching his sandwich.

"Yes, we did something like this almost every weekend. Mom would have the picnic basket ready when Dad got home, and we'd take off to a favorite spot. And we did a lot of camping too. I really loved doing that."

"You know, I never once had a family outing like you've described," he said, looking wistful. "That's why I enjoy being with you so much. You show me a side of life that I've always wanted, but never had."

Laurel stared at him, touched by his words.

"I'm glad," she finally responded.

His blue eyes held hers as he spoke again. "And I meant it when I said no one interests me as much as you. Frankly, I've never met a woman who captured my thoughts the way you have. When I'm in Atlanta, I'm constantly wishing I were here."

"The mountains—"

"No, Laurel," he interrupted, "it isn't just the mountains. It's you."

He reached forward and gripped her hand. "Each time I'm with you, I like you better than before. May I ask how you feel?"

Laurel dropped her eyes to the thermos of tea, wondering how to respond. She owed him honesty, she knew that; and yet, something deep in her soul held her back. *Is it pride,* she wondered, *or fear?*

"Sorry if I put you on the spot," he said, brushing the crumbs from his jeans. "Ready to go?" As he came to his feet, Laurel realized she had offended him.

She stood up and turned to him, slipping her arms around his waist. Suddenly she didn't care who passed them on the road, or if she were putting her heart on the line again.

"Matt, I do like you. Very much. It's just that—"

His lips swept over hers, silencing her objections, as she leaned against his chest, kissing him back. The late afternoon breeze wafted over them, bringing the freshness of evergreens and the coolness of the stream.

When she finally pulled back from him, smiling into his face, she took a deep breath. "We'd better go," she said, her eyes slipping over each feature of his face.

"Why?" he teased. "Are you worried about tarnishing the image of Teacher of the Year?"

She laughed, wondering who had told him about her award. "Not worried, exactly, but I wouldn't score any points with par-

ents who caught us smooching out here for all the world to see."
She sighed. "Actually, I thought we might like to get back to
Angel Valley before dark."

"Do the ghosts and goblins come out then?" He was still
hugging her against him, taunting her with his words and his
eyes.

She laughed, pounding his chest. "Stop teasing me!"

"All right, you win," he said, releasing her. "I suppose I'm
playing second fiddle to the Music Mountaineers again."

"No, to your sister. I promised to go by Ted Fisher's house
this evening in search of a special book on photography for her.
And I've already called him to say I'll be stopping in. Want to
come along?"

He sighed. "Not particularly. To tell you the truth, I could
use a good night's rest. I've been going on about three hours of
sleep since Friday."

She shook her head regretfully. "You're working too hard.
Or," she teased, "were you having nightmares about me?"

"I have only sweet dreams when it comes to you."

They laughed together as they gathered up their picnic items
and returned to the car.

On the way home, Laurel entertained him with stories of the
mountain people, legends handed down from one generation to
another. By the time they arrived at her house, Matt looked like a
different man. The haggard expression had disappeared from his
face, and he chuckled easily.

"When are you returning to Atlanta?" she asked.

He groaned. "Please, must you remind me?"

"Sorry."

"I'm not sure. While the attorneys work out the details on the sale of the shopping center, I may hang out here. Would you like that?"

She grinned. "Do you have to ask?" She reached for her purse and sweater. "Want to come in?"

"No, I'll let you go. Laurel, it was a great afternoon. Thanks for making it so special."

He reached out and pulled her to him for another kiss. This time he kissed her more fervently, and to her dismay, she responded the same way as the soft summer night wrapped around them. Breathlessly, she pulled away, turning for the door.

"Bye, Matt," she said, hopping out.

"You forgot something." He reached into the back seat for the picnic basket. "Keep it handy. I'd like to go again."

"That suits me fine," she called, then hurried up the walk to her house.

Although she had left lights on within the house, Laurel felt a sinking feeling as she entered. The house seemed dim and empty to her as she placed the basket on the kitchen table and removed the contents. Touching the empty containers, she recalled the things he had said to her and found herself staring into space, the thermos gripped against her chest.

With a sigh, she put the thermos in the sink then dropped into a chair, propping her elbows on the table. How could she bear the disappointment when he left for the winter? How could she go back to the same old routine? For she had come to realize how dull her life had been without Matt. And there was no way she could chalk this up as just a summer romance. She was falling for Matt, falling hard. There was no point in lying to herself. She thought she could keep a tight rein on her emotions, but that was before she got to know him, before she found a person who represented all she was looking for in a man. And yet...

She closed her eyes, wishing she could avoid the truth, but she couldn't. There were some terrible obstacles to overcome if their relationship were to last. His family, for starters. And their lifestyles. His work was in Atlanta; her work was in the valley. She had tried living in Atlanta, and she hated it. She had promised herself when she returned to Angel Valley that she would never leave again. She loved her work—and felt an unmistakable calling to remain—to teach these children what she knew about books and life.

Torn by conflict, she forced herself to head for her bedroom to shower and change clothes before going to Ted's house. It occurred to her, halfway between the kitchen and the bath, that she assumed there would be some need to make a change in her lifestyle. In all probability, there never would be; for in order for that to happen, she would have to....

She gulped at the thought. *I would have to marry Matt!*

She met her face in the mirror, and suddenly she paled visibly in the glow of the lamp's light. Marry Matt! Of course she couldn't marry Matt. She was leaping to conclusions; Matt would never ask her to marry him.

She sank onto the vanity stool, staring at her lips and remembering his kiss.

Laurel awoke to a soft gray drizzle beyond her bedroom window. She turned over in bed, burrowing deeper into her pillow and wanting to snuggle up, sleep another hour.

She opened one eye, squinting at the clock that sounded it's irritating alarm. Her arms wound around the pillow, hugging it against her, as she thought of Matt. Like a ray of sunshine, the thought of him brought a sparkle to the gloomy day. She smiled lazily. He was still here; maybe they could plan another picnic.

Suddenly energized by the thought, she bolted out of bed and dashed to the kitchen.

Later, arriving at Raven Ridge, she saw his car parked beside Madeline's in the driveway. However, after Lou opened the door for her, Anna Lee seemed to be the only person stirring. She sat on the sofa, absorbed in a book.

Laurel smiled to herself, pleased by the sight.

"Hi," she called. "Ready to get to work?"

Anna Lee smiled. "I suppose so."

It had been a simple, quiet day. Madeline did not put in an appearance, but Matt joined them briefly for lunch. He seemed in great spirits, and for once Anna Lee was pleasant and congenial in the company of her brother. Laurel was encouraged and decided maybe something might work out for her and Matt, after all.

After lunch, he excused himself, saying he had something to check on. With a lingering glance in Laurel's direction and a smile, he left the house. To her disappointment, he had not returned by the time she left for the day.

Despite the drizzling rain, Laurel decided to stop by the drugstore and have a chat with Rosemary.

"Where is everyone?" Laurel asked, looking around as she

entered. The store was practically empty with only Ellen, the pharmacist; Mr. White, the owner; and Rosemary, who served as bookkeeper and clerk, puttering about.

The social hour usually began sometime after three o'clock, when housewives stopped in before going to buy their groceries for the evening meal.

"Laurel!" Rosemary exclaimed, coming up from behind the counter where she was inspecting a new shipment of lipsticks. "Good. I can take a break."

"You just had a break," Mr. White called from behind the sports page of the Knoxville newspaper. An avid football fan, he was already making predictions about the Big Orange, come fall.

"She needs another break, Mr. White," Laurel called, as Mr. White lowered the paper a half inch, winked at her, then went back to his reading.

"Isn't he a laugh a minute?" Rosemary teased, hurrying around the counter.

"Rosie, have you heard anything from Jessica?" Laurel asked. "All I know about the wedding is that I'm supposed to wear the dress and shoes she sent and show up on time."

Rosemary frowned. "She called today, but she sounded frantic. She and Blake are winding up their jobs, coming here to get married, then going on to Florida. There'll be a rehearsal at the church Saturday evening, and the wedding is Sunday. She said Fanny is handling everything for her."

"Well, Fanny is equal to the task." Fanny was Rosemary's aunt. Aside from being organist at the church, she ran a small flower shop in Sevierville and helped with weddings.

"Jessica and Blake are opening a bed and breakfast in Florida," Rosemary said with a smile. "Doesn't that sound like fun?" She tilted her head and looked at Laurel, as though something had just occurred to her. "Sit down, Laurel. I'll make a trade with you." She motioned toward the soda fountain.

"What's the trade?" Laurel asked, settling onto the stool.

"Well...," she lowered her voice, "I'll trade you a soda for the story on a certain good-looking man. And what were you two doing on the front porch in the dark?"

The newspaper crackled behind them, and Laurel met Mr. White's eyes in the wall mirror. She swiveled around and looked at him. "She's just kidding, Mr. White."

"You going with that Wentworth fellow?" he asked, folding the newspaper into a neat square.

Laurel swallowed a deep sigh. If he were willing to pull his nose out of the sports page, local gossip must really be humming.

"I'm tutoring Anna Lee Wentworth, and naturally I'm friends with the family. Just friends," she repeated clearly as Rosemary draped over the counter and Ellen wandered up from the pharmacy.

"Hi, Laurel. How's it going?" Ellen smiled.

"Fine. And you?"

"Couldn't be better." Ellen was a perky redhead in her mid-thirties who had moved to Angel Valley with her husband and two sons. Weary of Alabama's humidity, they had come to the mountains to enjoy a better climate. Her husband taught all the math classes at the high school.

Laurel glanced back at Rosemary, dipping the ice cream scoop into the tub of vanilla. "Wait, Rosemary," Laurel spoke up. "I'll settle for a Diet Coke, please."

Rosemary grinned. "Suddenly watching your figure? Not that you ever needed to..."

The door opened and Mary Sue, the local beautician, entered. She was a trim brunette in her forties who worked hard at hanging onto her youth.

"Hi, Laurel, Rosemary, Ellen." She waved to Mr. White and settled onto a stool. "The thickest malt you can make, Rosemary," she grinned mischievously. "I'm celebrating the breakup with my boyfriend."

"Celebrating?" Ellen echoed.

"Now I can get off that ridiculous diet!" She focused on Laurel and moved over a stool to sit beside her. "What's he like? Everyone's dying to know."

Laurel fought a sting of irritation. No doubt she was this week's topic of conversation at the beauty shop, as well.

"They're only friends," Rosemary announced, placing the diet cola in front of Laurel.

"Friends!" Mary Sue hooted. "Nobody's going to fall for that one, Laurel. He's the most gorgeous man who ever got lost and ended up here. Every single woman in the county has been in to get her hair done! But I told the girls they're only dreaming; they don't stand a chance, even with the wonderful hairdos I create."

"That's just it," Laurel said coolly, "I don't stand a chance either. He's city; I'm country. We have nothing in common. That's why we're only friends," she finished smugly, giving Mary Sue a complacent little smile.

Mary Sue threw back her head and roared. "You don't fool me for a minute! *Friend* is the last word that comes to mind when I take a gander at him."

"Laurel's as pretty as any of those Atlanta floozies," Mr. White volunteered, reserve abandoned, as he strolled up to join the lively discussion.

Laurel pushed back her Coke. "I'm leaving if we don't change the subject."

Mr. White placed a hand on her shoulder, meeting her eyes in the wall mirror. "Maybe he'll become one of us," he offered reassuringly. "I hear he's looking around for a business to open up here."

Mary Sue whooped. "Wait'll my customers hear that. I'll make a fortune next week!"

Laurel was about to leave until Mr. White's words registered. "What kind of business?"

"Don't know. Someone said he'd been over to the mayor's office today. City council is having a meeting soon. Maybe he's gonna present a proposal."

"Well," Mary Sue lit a cigarette, "every female in town will be dressed to kill, and seated on the front row at that meeting. They may have a few proposals of their own ready for him." She snickered.

"Bye, ladies," Laurel called, waving as she headed for the door.

"I need to dash to the bank," Rosemary said, following Laurel outside. The rain had slackened, but it still was a gloomy day.

"Mary Sue makes me so mad," Laurel fussed, glancing at the sullen skies as Rosemary followed her to her car. "Why can't people tend to their own business?"

"Maybe because nobody has enough! We do lead pretty quiet lives, you know. When something new falls into our path, I'm afraid there are some who pounce like a dog on a soup bone. Forget what Mary Sue said."

Laurel frowned. "It's hard to forget. You know, one reason I'm upset is because Mary Sue is a reminder of the small town mentality here. We're mountaineers," she said glumly. "We have nothing in common with people like the Wentworths."

Rosemary groaned. "Stop that! Jim and I were impressed with Matt. He seems like a great guy, and he certainly went out of his way to be congenial to us after we horned in on your date."

"I'm glad you stopped by," Laurel said. "I wanted your opinion of him."

Laurel and Rosemary had been best friends throughout school, and remained as close as ever, even though Rosemary and Jim were inseparable when not at their jobs.

"Rosemary, I like Matt, but there's just no point in getting my hopes up," Laurel confided.

"Why not? You're intelligent and pretty and..."

Laurel put up a hand to silence her. "Different backgrounds, different lifestyles—remember sociology and the lesson Miss Carver pounded into our heads."

Rosemary smiled and leaned closer, whispering so that Fats, lumbering back to the drugstore, couldn't hear.

"Miss Carver was an old maid, remember? She might not have been so staunch about whom to pick for a husband if she'd ever had the chance. Some of those noble ideals go floating out the window when the right guy comes along."

Laurel turned and grinned at Rosemary. "You and Jim fell in love the minute you walked into freshman orientation at the university. And as far as I know, you two have never had a cross word. A marriage made in heaven. Not all of us are so blessed."

"Except for the babies we don't have," she said bleakly.

"I know." Laurel touched her hand and smiled. "Give yourself a little more time."

"Seems like five years is long enough." Rosemary's shoulders slumped as she spoke. "We may see a specialist in Knoxville."

"That's a wonderful idea. I know how you love kids, and you two will be great parents."

Rosemary gave Laurel a hug. "Thanks for the encouragement. You always make me feel better. Now you'd better get going before the rain starts again."

Laurel nodded, hopping into her car. "If you hear from Jessica, call me."

She drove off, thinking about Matt again. His face loomed in her memory, and a warm feeling crept over her, in spite of what she had just said to everyone about being friends. No, what she felt for Matt was *not* friendship.

To her disappointment, the phone did not ring as she made dinner for herself. She had washed up the dishes, put in a load of laundry, and checked intermittently to be sure the telephone was working. When she finally gave up on him, the phone rang and his voice came over the wire.

"Laurel, hi. I'm still here."

"Hi, Matt," she said, hopping onto the kitchen counter and nervously twirling the phone cord around her finger.

"Look, I have an idea," he was saying. "I want to see how you feel about it."

"Okay." She waited, eager to hear.

"How do you think people in Angel Valley would react to an arts center here? A tiny version of what we saw in Gatlinburg."

The idea took her completely by surprise. "Why, I don't know. I'd have to think about it."

"What's there to think about? It would give people—your

grandmother, for example—an outlet for their handiwork."

Laurel frowned. "Yes, but we're just simple folks, whereas the people over in Gatlinburg are skilled craftsmen."

"Maybe you're overlooking the gold in your own back yard. What about those rocking chairs I saw on your grandmother's porch? And her quilts? And those great-looking baskets that were displayed at the fair? I think there's some unique work right in your area, just waiting to be marketed."

Laurel stared through the rain-streaked window into the darkness. "The problem is, most of these people don't want to be 'marketed,' as you put it. They're happy with their lives."

"Come on, Laurel. Are you telling me they'd simply rather call their work a hobby and refuse money for it?"

"A few years back, a businessman from Knoxville proposed a consignment agreement with Harold for all his rockers. I'm not sure what happened, but Harold was unhappy with the outcome. He said he'd never get involved again with outsiders."

"That was one bad experience. Other people might not agree. Besides, that money could benefit the entire community." His voice softened. "I'm not proposing any drastic changes. I just thought it'd be great to try something that could bring in some money for the people."

Laurel sighed. "When you put it that way, the idea is more appealing. Matt, I'm not the right person to advise you."

"Why not? You're interested in arts and crafts; you're interested in the people in your community."

"Yes," she unclasped her ponytail and shook it loose, then plowed her fingers through the thick ends. "But I'm very protective of Angel Valley. Maybe that's selfish. Talk to Granny. She has a level head and a sense of what's right for everyone."

"Good suggestion. I'll do that. What's her telephone number?"

Laurel rattled it off, wondering as she did so, if she was doing the right thing. Still, it couldn't do any harm for Matt to have a chat with Granny. She was very wise.

"Laurel?" His voice drifted softly over the wires.

"Hmmm?"

"I'm staying the rest of the week, so I'd like to take you to dinner tomorrow night. And I won't take no for an answer."

She laughed. "I wasn't going to say no."

After they said goodbye and she hung up the phone, she stood staring into space.

What in the world was she going to do with Matt Wentworth? When she was with him, she could think of all the reasons it could work and why she wanted it to work. When she was away from him, she saw things quite differently. Realistically. The problem was, as Rosemary had so clearly pointed out, her heart didn't always react to logic and reason.

A gain Matt had been scarce at the house, and Laurel was relieved for that. She had given Anna Lee some tests to measure her progress, and both were delighted when her scores ranged from 82 to 95 in all of her subjects. For the first time, she wanted to see Madeline and tell her about the scores. When she mentioned this, Anna Lee merely shrugged.

"All she does lately is lie in bed and watch television."

"Be sure to tell her how well you're doing," Laurel prompted.

Anna Lee frowned. "Half the time she doesn't pay any attention to what I say to her."

Laurel thought that was very sad, but she kept her opinion to herself as she brought out the photography book she had located for Anna Lee, who lost all reserve and threw her arms around Laurel's neck. Laurel hugged her back, pleased by Anna Lee's show of affection.

That afternoon, when Laurel turned into her driveway, she spotted a piece of paper taped to the front door. She had been thinking of her dinner date with Matt and the sight of that note brought a sense of dread. Had he been called back to Atlanta?

Gathering up books and purse, she jumped out of the car and hurried up the steps. She smiled with relief as she recognized Granny's distinctive scrawl.

I'm baking a chocolate cake. Will expect you around four. With love, your super granny.

Laurel changed into comfortable clothes and hopped back in the car, heading to her grandmother's house.

When she rounded the curve, she was at first surprised to see Matt's Jeep parked in the driveway. Then she recalled their conversation on the telephone and realized that he had taken her suggestion about consulting Granny.

She parked her car and glanced into her rearview mirror. Because of the heat, she had braided her hair; it hung down her back like...*a true mountaineer,* she thought, grinning. A well-worn, Lee College T-shirt flared over white cotton shorts, revealing shapely legs that ended in scuffed tennis shoes worn without socks.

Grabbing her purse, she quickly applied fresh lip gloss and a dab of blush then hurried to the house. Laughter floated through the open door when she stepped onto the porch. She opened the screen and walked back to the kitchen where a luscious-looking chocolate cake sat in the center of the table, one chunk missing.

"We were just talking about you," Granny said, giggling.

She wore her usual jeans, with a perky red shirt. While her hair had that slightly tousled look, her eyes glowed and her skin held a light blush, as though she'd been standing over the stove or was in a state of excitement. Laurel glanced toward the stove, which was turned off, and correctly assumed the conversation, and the presence of Matt had Granny in what she would term a "tizzy."

He came to his feet, turning to smile at Laurel. "Well, hello," he said, pulling back a chair for her. He was casually dressed in a blue Oxford shirt over khaki slacks and loafers.

"Hello," her smile moved from Matt to Granny, slicing cake for her. "And just what were you two saying about me?"

"We were recalling what a good sport you were on the dunking machine," Matt said pleasantly.

"I imagine you were laughing at the way I came up sputtering and sloshing!" She reached for her cake.

"Take a bite of that," he said proudly, as though he had somehow assisted in the baking.

"Looks like another flop," she sighed, dipping the tip of her fork into the satiny icing. "Mmmm," she sighed, closing her eyes.

"Your grandmother and I have been having a great time." He straightened in his chair, glancing across at Granny. "I came to make an offer on some of her land."

The rich moist chocolate suddenly became a weight on Laurel's tongue. Her eyes shot to Granny, who watched her carefully.

"After I spoke with you last night," Matt continued, "I called and asked her opinion on an arts center here. Would you like to tell your granddaughter how you feel about it?"

Granny looked Laurel squarely in the eye. "I think it's a grand idea. A place for the local people to make a little money on the work they love to do."

Laurel was chewing slowly, listening, thinking. Her grandmother was always right. Why did she feel this strange apprehension that she couldn't define? She swallowed the cake, ran her tongue over her front teeth, and looked at Matt.

"And you want to put it on Granny's land, there along the highway?"

Matt smiled. "It's perfect, don't you agree?"

Laurel looked back at her grandmother. "You'd better think about this."

"I've already thought about it. Called both the boys and discussed it with them. They're agreeable."

Laurel fought against a vague pain beginning to settle around her heart. "You didn't call me," she said in a voice that seemed to come from deep in her chest.

Granny shook her head. "No, I didn't. Laurel, I know how you feel about this land, but I could use the extra money. I've been wanting new carpet for years, and the Asheville Carpet Outlet has that country blue on sale. It's exactly what I'd like to put throughout the house."

"But is it worth the privacy you'd be giving up? Do you really want to sit on your front porch and gaze at the people coming and going up there, with their horns blaring, engines roaring—"

"I want that carpet," Granny said dully, staring at the cake.

Automatically, Laurel's eyes drifted to the living room, seeing the frayed, out-of-date carpet. Of course Granny deserved to have something nice if she wanted it. But why couldn't her sons provide her with new carpeting, so that she wouldn't have to sell off her land? She turned back to her grandmother.

"Did you tell Uncle Frank and Uncle Bill that you needed new carpet? I'm sure they'd do that for you without your having to sell land, for heaven's sake." Laurel heard her voice rise even though she struggled to stay calm.

"Laurel, they have their own lives to live, children to educate, wives to care for. I don't expect anything from them."

"Well, you should!" Laurel threw down her napkin and paced the kitchen floor, ignoring Matt. "Dad would have bought you carpet. It's not fair. Your other sons never do anything to help you, while Dad...," she bit her lip, feeling the sting of tears.

"Your dad was a great blessing," Granny said quietly. "Yes, he was always here to fix the leaky faucet, patch the roof, clean the gutters. But I don't have him now."

Matt had come to his feet, looking at Laurel with a strange expression.

"I'm sorry, Laurel. I didn't know you'd be so upset."

"Because you didn't ask me! And frankly, I don't appreciate you coming to Granny about her land, taking advantage of her vulnerable situation, making an offer she can't refuse."

Anger clouded his features as she spoke, although he said nothing to her.

"Now just a minute," Granny said sternly, "you're being rude and unreasonable. There's nothing underhanded about his offer or his coming to see me. You told him to call me."

"Granny, he's a developer!" Laurel cried out. "He has no sense of how we live here or of what we want to preserve. He's in the business of making money—"

"Excuse me," Matt cut in. "The fact that I live in Atlanta and operate an investment business doesn't make me a shark, looking for someone to devour. Furthermore, I didn't know I was supposed to check with you before I spoke to your grandmother about her land." He turned to Granny, who looked miserable. "Thank you for the hospitality. I'd better go."

Laurel was determined to get in the last word. "As for our dinner date, I seem to have lost my appetite."

Without so much as a glance in her direction, he turned and hurried out of the house. Neither woman spoke as the Jeep roared off. Then Granny's voice cut through the silence that followed.

"Young lady, I can't remember ever seeing you behave worse."

Laurel sank into the chair, propped an elbow on the kitchen table, and cupped her chin in her hands.

Granny whisked away the dirty plates, grabbed up the cake, and took it to the cabinet. Laurel could see by the way she was darting around, slamming drawers, that she was angry. *Unlike me, she can at least hold her tongue,* Laurel thought dismally. But couldn't she see what was happening? Was she so blinded by Matt's charm that she was willing to sell the most precious thing that belonged to her?

Laurel cleared her throat, trying to calm her voice. "I'm sorry, but I just couldn't help it. He's been admiring your land ever since he first came out here. I should have known he was only interested in...," she broke off, biting her lip.

"Only interested in what?" Granny repeated, whipping off the water faucet. "Why don't you come out and say what's really bothering you, Laurel? You have this silly notion that he has to have some ulterior motive for wanting to date you, that he couldn't possibly appreciate you. After all, you're only a bright, warm, caring young woman who just happens to be a beauty."

"Spoken by a truly unbiased grandmother!" Laurel hooted, then gave a begrudging little smile. "Let's forget about me, for a minute. I do want what's best for you, even if I acted like a spoiled brat just now." She took a deep breath, and released it slowly. "Granny, if you really want to sell some land..."

"But I don't. Not anymore. It's not worth the hassle with you." She wiped her hands on a towel and came back to the table, slipping into the chair beside Laurel. "For you are the most important person in my life. There's no way I can do anything that would upset you."

Laurel reached over, giving the small woman a hug. "Granny, I just have a bad feeling about this; I can't explain why."

"Oh, I know why," Granny said, patting her hand, staring absently across the kitchen. "You're just like your father and grandfather. They wouldn't have wanted me to sell either." She was thoughtful for a few minutes before looking back at Laurel. "Maybe you're right. What does it matter about carpet?"

Laurel swallowed. "It matters a lot if you want it that badly. But give me time. I'll see that you have new carpet, Granny, I promise; and anything else you want, if I can humanly get it for you."

Granny smiled. "Let's forget it. What does concern me, Laurel, is that you may be overlooking an opportunity for other people here. I know for a fact there are people who would be in favor of a place where they could sell their work. And you know that some of them desperately need the money. Why, Harold could do well with his rockers!"

"Remember the businessman from Knoxville? Harold said he never would try again to—"

"That was before Sadie developed cancer," Granny cut in. "Now, they're in a terrible bind. I think he would trust someone like Matt. And they certainly need the money."

Laurel closed her eyes, as a wave of guilt swept over her. "I'm sorry. I have been selfish. But Granny," she looked deeply into her grandmother's eyes, "I've lived where people have to lock all their doors, where some women even carry guns to protect themselves. Not to mention the traffic and the pollution. Is it selfish to want to protect the people I love? I know what a treasure we have in this quiet little valley. It's fresh and unique, and I guess I'm just so afraid it will get spoiled."

Granny nodded. "I understand. But remember other people have a right to make that decision, as well."

Laurel sighed. "Do you want Angel Valley covered with tourists?"

Granny shook her head. "I don't relish that thought. On the other hand, I don't think it's quite right to hoard our pretty little community, denying others the pleasure of coming in to see how we conduct our lives, do our work, raise our families, and hold onto our faith. Maybe they'd learn something of value from us."

"Oh, they could learn a lot from us," Laurel answered quickly, then pressed her lips together.

It was no use trying to make Granny understand. She hadn't fought five o'clock traffic in a city, or had to go for allergy shots because of pollution in the air. And Matt was a very charming man. A sharp pain tore at her heart as she recalled their argument, the set of his jaw when he left. Well, it was time they got this out in the open. Now, she'd see how many times he called!

She pulled herself up out of the chair. "I have to go. Are you coming to the wedding on Saturday?"

Granny nodded, but she didn't seem to be listening to what Laurel had to say about a wedding. "I hate for you to leave."

Laurel reached down to hug her again. "I apologize again if I've upset you."

"Never mind. I still think Matt Wentworth means well and

that he's not out to develop our little community."

Laurel held her tongue on the subject. "Goodbye, Granny. See you in a day or two."

She went out to her car and fell into the front seat, all energy drained from her body. As she backed out of the drive and drove along the highway, she thought of Matt's offer to buy the land. She hadn't even asked what he was willing to pay!

Anger surged through her again as she glanced out across the peaceful green meadows and thought of her father and her grandfather. They'd be furious if they knew what he had tried to do. She was glad she'd stood her ground; someone had to do that. Granny was no match for a shrewd businessman like Matt Wentworth. And that's what he was, she saw that now. No matter what he said about the advantage to the community, he was seeing dollar signs. Why else was he so interested? And in his own way, she suspected he loved money every bit as much as his mother did, who demanded a jet at her disposal, a cook at the ready, private schools and tutors, anything to make life more comfortable.

She drove home feeling totally miserable.

The sound of Jessica's happy voice over the telephone that evening lifted her spirits.

"Laurel, I can't wait to see you!" Jessica bubbled.

As Laurel listened to Jessica detail her wedding plans, Laurel recalled how she and Rosemary had always teased that Jessica was the one with the class.

"Jessica, I wish you had more time here. We'll hardly get to visit," Laurel complained.

"We'll make the most of it," Jessica promised. "Then you guys will have to come to Florida to see us; you can bask in the

160

sun while I wait on you hand and foot!"

They laughed together, then returned to last-minute details about the wedding. After Laurel hung up, she sank into a chair and stared at the floor.

Rosemary was happy. Jessica was happy. Why couldn't she find happiness?

The next day as she drove to the Wentworth house, Laurel felt as though her nerves were tangled up like a wad of spaghetti. She couldn't bear the thought of another encounter with Matt, particularly if Madeline were around to hear and gloat! With any luck he had returned to Atlanta, and she would avoid him.

Those hopes fell flat as soon as her little car topped the steep incline and she spotted his Jeep parked beside Madeline's Mercedes.

A door slammed somewhere at the rear of the house, and she jumped and made a grab for her books and purse. She was just getting out of the car when Matt rounded a corner of the house, striding toward his Jeep.

She froze, wondering if she should pretend not to see him or make a dash for the walk, as though she were late for work. She was early, in fact; and she'd have to be blind not to see him.

His eyes met hers at that moment, and she stopped breathing. He didn't appear inclined to offer her a good morning, so she decided to follow suit. Turning on her heel, she headed up the walkway, both too proud to speak first.

Numbly, she entered the house, giving Lou a bland smile and making the appropriate comments while her mind lingered on Matt.

"Hi," Anna Lee said.

Laurel placed her load on the coffee table, and straightened.

"Hi."

"Well, aren't you going to say anything?" Anna Lee asked.

"Hmmm?" Laurel walked toward a chair and turned to look at her student.

"Do you like my new outfit?"

"Oh," Laurel blurted, as her eyes ran down the pale blue slacks and matching shirt, which she assumed were new. "I do like it. You look great."

Anna Lee sidled up to Laurel, her dark eyes shining. "I've lost seven pounds," she said under her breath, as though afraid to admit it to anyone.

"Anna Lee, that's wonderful! I had noticed a change," Laurel touched her arm. "I'm proud of you. I hope you'll be encouraged by your progress and keep at it."

Anna Lee nodded. "Mother has promised to buy me another camera and lots of film," she stated proudly. "I told her about the pictures I took yesterday and how much fun we had."

Laurel smiled, pleased to see Anna Lee looking happy. She didn't even mind when Laurel gave her another quiz.

When Lou announced lunch, she and Anna Lee headed to the dining room, while Laurel sneaked a glance toward the driveway. She couldn't see the cars from the window, but she prayed Matt had returned to Atlanta and she wouldn't be forced to face him again. Maybe, just maybe, she and Anna Lee could dine alone.

While Matt didn't show up for lunch, to Laurel's surprise, Madeline did. It was the first time she had chosen to accompany them since reprimanding Laurel for taking Anna Lee to church.

"May I join you?" she asked casually.

"Of course," Laurel forced a smile.

"Lou is trying a new fish recipe, and I wanted to sample it."

"Fish?" Anna Lee said with a grimace, then caught herself as she glanced at Laurel.

Lou entered with the tray and served the food.

Madeline cleared her throat. "Anna Lee showed me the theme she wrote. I thought it was good." She was looking at her daughter with eyes that seemed to plead for friendship.

"She's doing very well," Laurel agreed. She so wanted to see mother and daughter united, sharing a friendship. They both seemed to need that desperately. "We're reviewing all her subjects, working on any area that troubles her."

Anna Lee sighed. "I'd rather take another field trip."

"Oh, we will," Laurel smiled.

"Since Anna Lee is doing well, I've decided to take a long weekend, since the Fourth of July falls on Monday. We're going to Atlanta until Tuesday. The plane is coming to pick us up this afternoon. We'll call you when we return," Madeline looked across at Laurel.

"I told you I don't want to go," Anna Lee pouted.

"Remember, we're going shopping for that camera and more film. Perhaps we'll investigate a photography class for you this fall. And besides, dear, I need to see my doctor and get my medicine refilled." Madeline had picked up her fork and speared the fish, baked to perfection and dusted with paprika. "This is good," she pronounced as Lou hovered in the background, her hands folded over her apron.

"Yes," Laurel smiled at Lou. "This is the best fish I've ever tasted." Laurel knew the cook tried hard to please everyone.

At Laurel's words, Lou's tense mouth fell into a broad smile. "Thank you."

Laurel relaxed when she realized that Matt would not be joining them. For once she actually enjoyed a meal while sitting at the same table with Madeline. She was again grateful for small blessings.

After class, Laurel said goodbye to Anna Lee. "Have fun in Atlanta," she said, giving her a hug.

"I don't want to go," Anna Lee muttered under her breath.

Laurel nodded, then thought of something. "I have a friend coming for a visit. He's a professional photographer. Maybe you'd like to meet him."

Anna Lee's eyes widened. "Sure."

"I'll ask him to come over when you get back, and give you some points on photography. So go on to Atlanta and get what you need."

Laurel left Anna Lee with happy thoughts; she wished she felt the same. *Have to take the bitter with the sweet*, she thought, reminding herself of what she had said to Anna Lee.

When she stopped in at the post office on her way home, Millie waved a letter from her mother.

"Thanks," Laurel said, tearing into the envelope. The words she'd been so eager to read now fluttered illegibly before her at Millie's next words.

"That Wentworth fellow was just in here," she said, watching Laurel's expression, "and guess who I saw out in the car with him?"

Laurel looked up from the letter, desperately wishing she could resist asking, but she couldn't. "Who?"

"Cheryl. She's back in town for the Fourth of July festivities."

There was only one Cheryl—long-legged, shapely, with thick auburn hair. Her father was the mayor of Angel Valley and she was, by far, the most sophisticated product the town could contribute to Chicago.

Laurel dropped her eyes to the letter in her hand, desperately hoping Millie would let it go, but of course she didn't.

"Mary Sue saw Matt Wentworth's car parked in front of the mayor's house, then the next thing you knew they were riding around town together."

Laurel couldn't take any more. Quickly folding the letter, she turned for the door. "They should make a good pair," she called over her shoulder, slamming the door behind her.

Cheryl did some modeling in Chicago, or so she told everyone, although no one had seen her picture in the many magazines she boasted of working for. Still, she loved city life, and, after all, her father was the mayor. *Yes, they should make a good pair. Maybe with the mayor's help, Matt and Cheryl could turn Angel Valley into a cheap little Chicago, and both would be happy.*

She jumped in the car and headed home, staring blankly through her windshield. She didn't even see him behind her, or hear the siren for a full ten seconds before he turned it up a notch.

Laurel jumped. Her eyes shot to her rearview mirror.

"Oh no," she groaned, as the blue light blinked at her, and Deputy Jasper Colburn pulled her over.

She braked and cut to the side of the road. Gravel spun around her.

Jasper got out, shaking his head at her as though she were a naughty child who deserved a spanking.

She thrust her head out the window. "Jasper, I have to get home right away."

"Laurel, I've told you before. You can't go ripping down the highway like that, endangering people's lives." He leaned through the window, warming to his speech. "We can't take the law in our own hands," he said, standing again, thrusting out his chest, obviously feeling important.

Laurel wondered how long it had been since he'd had the pleasure of reeling off his speech, watching someone squirm. She could tell him to come off it, or she could cower down and escape a speeding ticket. The last thing she wanted to do was kowtow to Jasper who had sat behind her in fifth grade, yanking her ponytail. Her dad had tried to soothe her when she complained about Jasper.

"Little boys have odd ways of showing their affection," her father had said to her as he sat in the recliner, puffing his pipe.

She knew, as the years passed, that Jasper had kept his crush a secret. Then, thankfully, Cindy got rid of her braces and went to contact lenses and Jasper had fallen madly in love. They eloped the night after graduation.

"Jasper," she took a deep breath, "I appreciate the warning. But right now," she turned her eyes upward, trying to look humble, "I just can't afford to pay a ticket. You know I'm trying to save money for a trip to Europe. Come on, Jasper. I won't do it again."

Jasper stared down at her, momentarily entranced. Then he squared his shoulders and nervously glanced around to see who had witnessed the chase. No one had. "Just be more careful..."

Laurel smiled. "Thanks for understanding. Listen, Jasper, if you want to catch a rich speedster, search for a black Jeep with a Georgia license plate."

His eyebrows shot to his hairline. "That city slicker Cheryl's riding around with?"

Laurel nodded. "They just passed me like a bat out of...you know where."

Jasper whirled, stretching his short legs into an odd sprint. *No wonder he never made the football team,* Laurel thought, frowning after him.

"Thanks for the tip," he yelled back.

Through the mirror, she saw the patrol car careening off in the opposite direction, blue light blazing. *All right, so it was a lousy thing to do.* But she just couldn't help it.

By the time she reached her driveway, she was laughing so hard that tears rolled down her cheeks. Then, as she sat there staring at her empty house, her laughter faded. The tears still trailed down her cheeks, but there was no joy behind them.

Eleven

Laurel sat at her kitchen table, staring disinterestedly through the window at a beautiful Saturday morning. She took another sip of sassafras tea, hoping Granny was right about how it cured all ills. She wondered, staring into the tea, if it could heal a broken heart.

Silly, she chided herself, *you're being as melodramatic as Jasper.* At the thought of Jasper chasing after Matt and Cheryl, she felt a stab of guilt. *You shouldn't have done that.* Turning to the shelf beside her table, she pulled down her Bible and a devotional book. As her hand brushed her Bible, she noticed the piece of paper tucked between the pages. She opened the back of the Bible and gently unfolded the paper. She had forgotten to give Anna Lee the verses she had promised her.

"God is my refuge and strength, a present help in time of trouble..."

A knock on her front door interrupted her reading. She laid down the Bible, glancing at her T-shirt and shorts. Her heart was already beating faster, and she found herself thinking of Matt as she hurried to the living room. Glancing through the window, she saw an unfamiliar sports car parked at the curb.

She opened the door to face Will Hargate, grinning from ear to ear. It was a different Will than she remembered, however; and for a moment, she could only stare at him.

The thin gangly boy she had grown up with had filled out considerably. While he was still thin, he no longer looked totally out of proportion with his six-foot frame. A ponytail had been added, along with an earring. She couldn't believe it. He still wore glasses, but the horn rims had been replaced by thin wire frames.

"Will! Come in!" He wore nice jeans with a blue button-down shirt and a pair of leather hiking boots that looked brand new.

"Hi, Laurel. It's great to see you."

As she opened the door, he leaned down to kiss her on the cheek. She put her arms around him, giving him a quick hug. She really was glad to see him; Will had become a part of their family, and there had been lots of good times. Those memories came rushing back now as she peered up through the wire rims to his gentle gray eyes.

"Will, I've missed you! How do you like New York?"

"I love it."

"What? My soulmate of the mountains loves the big city?"

He shrugged, looking shy, reminding Laurel for the first time of the boy she had grown up with.

"Just kidding," she said gently. "Congratulations on your new project. How long will you be here?"

"A few weeks."

"Then you must make the most of your time! Hey, I have an idea. Why don't we ride over to Pigeon Forge and get a jump on Christmas?"

"Christmas?" His eyebrows lifted.

"You know how you and Granny and I used to go over there Christmas shopping whenever we got bored. It always thrilled me to go in that Christmas store and see the trees lit up in June."

"Yeah," he said, laughing. "Let's go."

"Want to invite Granny to come along?"

"When I left the house, she was hosting a quilting bee," Will said. "This must be the last place in the world where they still do that!"

"Oh, I doubt it."

"The women came before I got up. They had that dining room table covered with a hundred scraps of cloth."

Laurel laughed. "They'll be at it all day, talking, eating. They really enjoy themselves."

Will grinned. "I'd forgotten how food is so much a part of everything here. It's a wonder more people aren't overweight."

"They get their exercise clogging! Haven't you missed all the crazy fun around here?"

He nodded. "I have." His eyes lingered on the table, and she saw that he was staring at her Bible. A strange expression crossed his face, and Laurel wondered what he was thinking.

"Have you found a church up there?"

He looked across the room at her, shaking his head. She expected him to elaborate on her question, but he fell silent.

"Well," she said, when he didn't seem inclined toward further conversation, "I'll just freshen up and we'll be on our way."

Hours later, with packages in hand, they emerged from the twinkling lights of the Christmas shop in Pigeon Forge.

"Where do all these people come from?" Will groaned, as they got back in his car and waited for an opening in traffic.

"Oh come on," Laurel laughed, "you live in New York, remember? The traffic may bottleneck here now and then, but it's still a fun place. Everyone loves bargains, and we have outlets galore. And there's Dollywood and the Music Mansion...," her voice trailed, as she glanced up and down at all the shops and restaurants. "Want to eat at the Apple Barn?"

Over a delicious meal, Laurel and Will caught up on each other's lives over the past years.

"You really should come up to New York to visit me," Will said as he paid the bill.

"I might do that sometime," Laurel answered. They turned a corner and came face to face with Matt and Cheryl having dinner.

Dressed in a white silk pants suit, Cheryl was stunning. Her short auburn hair curled around her face, emphasizing perfect skin and clear green eyes. Laurel glanced again at Matt, and their eyes held.

"Hello you two!" Cheryl called out. "Will, you look totally different!"

"So do you," he responded with a smile.

"Well, it has been a few years, hasn't it? Hello, Laurel."

"Hello." Laurel forced a smile.

"Will, I'd like you to meet Matt Wentworth." Cheryl gave Matt a brilliant smile. "Matt, this is Will Hargate."

As the men shook hands, Laurel watched Matt's eyes travel

up and down Will, returning to the earring, then the ponytail. Slowly, his gaze moved back to Laurel and his eyes darkened.

Cheryl looked at Laurel, then Matt. "You two have already met, haven't you?"

"Yes, we have," Matt replied stiffly.

"Will, I hear you've hit the big time," Cheryl ran on breathlessly. "You know Angel Valley—no secrets there. Tell me about New York."

"I like it," he said quietly. "I think that came as a surprise to Laurel." There was no mistaking the affection in his eyes when he looked at her.

Laurel smiled blankly. She sneaked another glance at Matt while Cheryl launched into a series of questions about New York. Matt looked from Will to Laurel.

Laurel cleared her throat. "Matt, did you find another spot for your project?"

"No, I've shelved that particular project."

Laurel considered his words, and wondered if Granny, and everyone else, would blame her for spoiling plans for the art center.

"Maybe I'll come up for a visit sometime," Cheryl said to Will. "My company has offered to send me up there on a modeling assignment."

"Then please look me up," Will said, then glanced at Matt. "Nice meeting you."

Matt nodded briskly. "You, too."

As they left the restaurant and walked down the steps to the parking lot, Will looked at Laurel. "Cheryl turned into a real beauty, didn't she?"

Laurel tried to squelch her jealousy. "Yep, she did."

"Is that the 'Matt' Granny told me about?"

Laurel took a deep breath. "There's only one."

As the lights in the parking lot settled over Laurel's features, Will turned and looked at her thoughtfully. He reached into his pocket for the car keys, asking nothing else, and she was more grateful for his silence than he would ever know.

She felt sick at heart, almost sick to her stomach, in fact. The old problem with her ulcer was definitely returning.

"Ready to go home?" he asked, opening the car door for her.

She nodded. "More than ready." Seeing the look of disappointment on his face, she quickly added, "Aren't you tired?"

"Not really. But it's getting late."

She pressed her head against the seat, thinking of the Fourth of July barbecue in the town park on Monday. She couldn't bear to see Matt with Cheryl again; maybe she'd just stay home.

Laurel put on a brave smile for her Sunday activities, beginning with the lively five-year-olds in Sunday school. As she sat with Granny in church, she was grateful that her grandmother kept the conversation away from Matt and his offer to buy her land.

"Want to come home with me for lunch?" Granny asked. "Will is there, puttering around."

Laurel shook her head. "I think I'll ride up to Knoxville and do some shopping. I need some new shoes."

Granny patted her hand. "A shopping trip will be good for you. Buy whatever you need, and a few things you don't."

They laughed at that, remembering in past years when Granny would press some "fun" money in her hand and say, "buy something you want but don't need. It's good for the soul."

As Laurel looked at Granny, remembering those times now, she felt she had deprived her grandmother of the new carpet, which she both needed *and* wanted. She reached over and hugged her grandmother.

Shopping at the mall was simply no fun at all. Just before dark, Laurel returned home. As she unlocked the door, she could hear the telephone ringing. She hurried inside, dumping her packages, but by the time she reached the phone, the caller had hung up.

Flopping into the chair, she stared at the fern and thought of Matt. Would he ever call her again? And did she want him to? As much as she hated to admit the truth, she missed him. He kept creeping into her thoughts, wherever she went, whatever she did. And she was surprised at how much it hurt to think their relationship was over.

The phone rang again, startling her out of her depression. This time she grabbed it on the second ring.

"Laurel, you're supposed to be saving your money for Europe. You shouldn't have bought this carpet!" Granny admonished.

"Carpet?" Laurel echoed. "What are you talking about?"

There was a brief silence. "You mean you didn't have all this carpet delivered? You didn't go to Asheville, pick it out, and pay for it?"

Laurel was bewildered. "No, I didn't."

"Well, a truck pulled up and at first, I thought there'd been a mistake. Then I saw my name was on the delivery slip. And it's that country blue I've been wanting."

Laurel sank into the kitchen chair. "I had nothing to do with it. Would Uncle Frank or Uncle Ben have—"

"No, but I'll bet I know who did. Remember how I went on about that carpet when Matt was here, named the store and the pattern? And who else could pay to have it delivered on a Sunday afternoon? I should have known! I'll have to call him and refuse—"

"No, don't do that. I mean, if it's already been delivered." She thought for a minute. "We'll pay him for it. Oh, Granny," she wailed, closing her eyes. "He's probably just trying to get even with me."

"Laurel, how can you be so suspicious? He is a very nice guy, but you want to pin all kinds of ulterior motives on him."

Laurel's head throbbed as she tried to figure things out.

"Granny, please call him. Tell him the carpet was a nice gesture but we intend to pay for it." She bit her lip. "Maybe you should sell the land to him, after all." She hadn't the courage to tell her grandmother that Matt had shelved the project.

"Why can't you call him?" Granny persisted.

"Because we aren't on good terms and because Will and I saw him with Cheryl in Pigeon Forge yesterday." Her head pounded as her thoughts flew in all directions.

"Maybe I'll just wait and speak to him tomorrow," Granny said. "I reckon he'll be at the barbecue, don't you?"

Laurel gritted her teeth, fighting the headache and the thought of seeing him again. With Cheryl. "I don't know. Granny, I have to go." She hung up and searched for the aspirin bottle. Not only had she messed everything up for the creative people in Angel Valley, she'd lost him to Cheryl. Not that she wanted him. Or did she?

By the next morning Laurel had devised a plan. She'd go to the bank and get a loan to pay for the carpet. But first she'd speak to Matt and ask him how much he'd paid for it so she would know how much to borrow. Then, she would calmly assure Matt that he'd have his money in a few days.

Strengthening her resolve, Laurel dressed carefully, putting on the new floral sundress she had purchased. She stood before the mirror and checked her makeup.

Although her eyes were dark-circled, her hair gleamed from the morning's shampoo, and the blush and lip gloss offset the pallor of her skin. She slipped her feet into sandals, made a turn in front of the mirror, and decided that she passed inspection.

She grabbed her car keys and sailed out the front door, determined to make amends if at all possible.

The park overflowed with people, and Laurel quickly spotted Cheryl, selling raffle tickets at the Lions Club booth. Laurel looked around, expecting Matt to be hovering close by, but he was nowhere in sight.

"I don't see him either," Granny said from behind her.

Laurel jumped and whirled. Her grandmother wore a new pair of jeans and a white shirt. Packages of napkins and paper plates exploded from her arms.

"He hasn't been here at all," she said, and lowered her voice. "And Cheryl came alone."

176

"Where's Will?" Laurel asked, suddenly remembering that he was staying at Granny's house.

"He decided he'd rather go over to Cades Cove." Granny's eyes twinkled. "He still gets nervous in a crowd."

"Then how does he live in New York?" Laurel asked absently, as her eyes swept parents, children, stray dogs, and a group of widows standing together, all talking at once.

"Folks in the big city are strangers to him; they don't bother him. These folks remember when he was a skinny little guy in ragged overalls. And I suspect he's self-conscious about his ponytail around here. I don't care for it and told him so."

"Granny, it's his life. Let's let him live it. I'll see you later."

Laurel circled the outer edge of the crowd, satisfied that Matt was not present. If he was at the barbeque, he would be with Cheryl. *Maybe he's still at Raven Ridge,* she thought.

As she drove to the mansion, she mentally prepared her little speech. All she had to do was keep a cool head, but her resolve evaporated when her car topped the incline and she saw his Jeep parked in the driveway.

Keep your mind on your mission, she warned herself, as she got out and slammed the door. The sound brought Matt around the corner of the house.

Good. She could talk with him out in the yard, which she thought would be easier than inside the house.

"Hi," she called, trying to sound normal. "Got a minute?"

"Sure."

She noticed then that he was dressed in shorts, a faded T-shirt and sneakers. *He must not be planning to go to the barbecue, after all.*

177

"I can't stay," she began, crisscrossing her fingers in front of her sundress.

His blue eyes peered down into her face, and his head was tilted as though wondering what she was up to. "Fine, but can we talk around back? I'm kind of in the middle of something."

She saw that he held a brush with traces of soap suds. She nodded, following him around the corner of the house to the back yard where, to her astonishment, a golden retriever puppy was hunkered down in a big washtub.

"Oh, how sweet!" she cried, hurrying to kneel down beside him. "What's his name?"

"I think I'll call *her* Penny."

Laurel's eyes danced as she looked from Matt back to the puppy's copper fur and nodded. "I can see why." She reached forward to pet the damp little head. "Where did you get her?"

"Believe it or not, she was wandering around down there on the highway. She wore no collar, and her fur was matted and dirty. I can't believe someone just dumped her out. Anyway, she looked hungry, and I couldn't just leave her."

Laurel's eyes filled with wonder as he spoke, and suddenly her image of the cold, hard businessman dissolved as she turned back to the puppy. Maybe Granny was right about him simply trying to help folks in Angel Valley.

She sat back on her heels, staring at the dog's big brown eyes, until the memory of Cheryl and Matt cozied up for dinner in Pigeon Forge lurched back to haunt her. She felt a cloud of gloom settling over her again.

"What did you want to talk about?" he asked, kneeling down, dipping the brush in the sudsy water.

She sighed. "The carpet! It was a very thoughtful thing for you to do, but we can't accept it. I mean, I want Granny to keep the carpet, but the only way she'll do that is for us to pay for it, and we can. Matt, I won't hear of anything else."

He looked over the puppy's damp back to where Laurel crouched, one hand still stroking the puppy's silky fur. "What are you talking about?" he asked.

She stared for several seconds. "We assumed...," she gulped, "I mean, didn't you go over... I assumed you called the outlet in Asheville and had them deliver that carpet Granny mentioned when you were there."

He ran the brush over the puppy's body, grinning as Penny licked his hand. Finally, his blue-gray eyes returned to Laurel.

"I didn't call any carpet places."

"Then you went..."

"Nope. Sorry."

She stared at him in disbelief. Her eyes fell to the puppy, and suddenly she felt more foolish than she'd ever felt in her life.

If he didn't call, who did? And more importantly, he must think this sounded like the most ridiculous story he'd ever heard—one she had probably trumped up as an excuse to see him again! Her cheeks flamed with humiliation.

She took a deep breath and stood up, dusting off her skirt.

"Well, apparently one of my uncles has done something nice, after all. Sorry to have bothered you."

He said nothing as he continued to bathe the puppy.

"Nice meeting you, Penny," she said, scratching the dog's wet head, and then turned to go.

"Wait." He laid the brush down and dried his hands. "I've

just made up some lemonade. I'll get us a glass."

She hesitated, glancing around for the first time. She could see a white wicker table and chairs grouped around a barbecue grill at the opposite end of the house. Maybe they did need to talk.

"Want to baby-sit while I grab the drinks and a big towel to wrap her in?"

She smiled at the puppy and knelt to pet her again. "Sure."

As she stared into the puppy's soulful eyes, she decided that Matt had to have a tender heart in order to rescue an abandoned puppy and care for her. It seemed odd that he was here, all by himself, bathing a puppy when he could be with Cheryl.

Soon he was back, carrying a large bath towel and two glasses, which he placed on the table.

"Better stand back," he said, his eyes traveling over her sundress. "You look too pretty to get drenched."

She retreated to the table then laughed as he lifted the wiggling puppy from the tub and water sprayed in all directions.

"I'm going to put her upstairs in the bathroom so she'll stay dry. And clean," he said directly to the puppy, whose tail flipped wildly as they disappeared into the house.

Laurel took a deep breath and settled into the cushions on the white wicker chair. As she sipped the lemonade, she closed her eyes and felt her taut nerves begin to relax.

The back door closed and his footsteps hurried over the stones. She opened her eyes as he approached her. His head was tilted slightly, and his eyes held a thoughtful expression.

"What is it?" she asked, before she thought.

He reached for his glass. "You're very pretty."

"I'm very rude! I want to apologize for behaving so badly at my grandmother's house the other day." Her eyes followed him as he sank into a chair opposite her. "I guess I go a little crazy when I think about Granny selling her land." She looked gravely at Matt. He was sipping his lemonade, listening intently as she spoke. "Perhaps I should have stayed out of it."

"Doesn't matter now," he said, looking at his glass. His thumb trailed a drop of lemonade down the side of the glass as his voice flowed into the quiet around them. "I've changed my mind about pursuing that particular project. Perhaps it wasn't a good idea, after all." He looked back at her, his eyes darkening.

Laurel tried to choose her words, stalling for time as she took another sip of lemonade. "I don't want to be the cause of folks not having something they want or need."

He pursed his lips, looking across at her. "Maybe I'll think about it again later. Right now, I have another project in mind, and once I zero in on something, it's hard for me to focus on anything else."

She wanted to inquire what the project was, but she knew she'd overstep her bounds.

"I'm curious," he said, leaning forward. "Hasn't there ever been anything you wanted to do for these people? Not that you don't do anything," he amended. "I know you're a very good teacher, and you do help in other ways."

"Like climbing on the dunking machine?" she teased.

He laughed at that, and she was relieved to feel the tension breaking between them.

"Oh, I know what you mean," she said, absently studying the crushed ice in her glass. "And I wish there was a way to do something without changing the town."

He looked at her thoughtfully. "Got any ideas?"

She shrugged. "Not at the moment."

He glanced at his watch, and suddenly Laurel wondered if she were interrupting something.

"I don't want to detain you if you have to be somewhere," she said, watching his expression.

He lifted his broad shoulders in a light shrug. "Well, to tell you the truth, I asked Cheryl out tonight."

"I see," she said, placing the glass on the table, coming quickly to her feet.

"Look, you were with that hippie on Saturday and—"

"Will is not a hippie!" she flared back. "And besides, people don't use that word anymore."

"Well, pardon me for being politically incorrect. But I assumed—"

"You assumed wrong. Will is only a friend," she said, tilting her head back and regarding him coolly. "A very good friend. But you'd better watch your step with Cheryl. She's broken many a heart."

"She won't break mine," he said quietly, as his eyes ran over her features, lingering on her lips.

He looked at her differently, and before she knew quite how it happened, he leaned forward and kissed her. The warmth of his lips was a jolt to her senses, and it was several seconds before she could break away.

They stared at one another, both at a loss for words, until he lifted his eyes to the mountains and took a deep breath.

"I'm sorry," he said softly. "I wish we had more time. I'm leaving for Atlanta first thing in the morning. And there are a few things I'd like to explain."

If he were going to explain why he had asked Cheryl out, there was certainly no mystery to that; still, her pride wouldn't allow her to hear anything more about another woman. Especially a woman as pretty and sophisticated as Cheryl.

"Maybe some other time," she said shakily, as she turned on her heel and hurried around the house, back to her car.

That evening, watching the fireworks from her front porch, she felt as lonely and dejected as the sad little bird, singing a night song in the pine tree at the corner of her house.

"I know, I feel the same way," she moaned, staring at the colors cascading over the navy sky. She couldn't bear to think about Matt being with Cheryl; it was the reason she had decided not to return to the park. In the distance she could hear voices rising and falling merrily as another rainbow of color exploded into the heavens. Were Matt and Cheryl watching the fireworks from his patio, drinking some of his famous lemonade? Or were they mixing with the townsfolk, charming everyone?

It had been such a strange afternoon that she didn't know what to think. As they sat together, sipping lemonade, Laurel had thought Matt looked at her as though he really did care for her. Or maybe she was just doing some wishful thinking.

One thing she did know. When she was with him, she felt an exquisite happiness; when she was not, she felt empty and incomplete.

She turned to look toward the starry heavens, thinking it was time she had a serious talk with God.

Twelve

"Granny, it's true. Matt didn't buy that carpet for you," Laurel argued into the telephone. "Must have been Uncle Frank or Uncle Bill."

"Maybe." Granny didn't sound convinced.

"You don't think they did," Laurel said quietly.

"If you didn't do it, and Matt didn't do it, I reckon it has to be my one of my boys, even though they're denying it."

"You have a birthday coming up. Bet Uncle Frank will admit to it then. You know how he likes pranks; he just wants to keep you guessing."

"Mmm-hmmm. So I'll just consider this a blessing from God and quit fretting," Granny concluded.

"Good idea," Laurel agreed. They said goodbye.

She knew Granny shared her suspicion that Matt Wentworth was somehow to blame or to thank.

On Tuesday morning, Anna Lee called to say they wouldn't be returning until the end of the week. She sounded so despondent that Laurel quickly promised her a field trip upon her return.

"I'll call you as soon as we get back," Anna Lee replied, sounding a bit more cheerful.

With another day to kill, Laurel vented her frustration by cleaning house. Then she baked up a batch of chocolate chip cookies, her favorite treat.

She was sitting on the porch step, munching away, when Will's sports car pulled into her driveway. She waved as he got out of the car, a sack tucked under his arm.

"Hi. You're just in time for cookies," she called to him.

"Good for me," he said, giving her that slow, shy grin.

As he crossed the yard, Laurel studied his long thin frame. One thing had not changed about Will: his walk. She and Granny had once decided he reminded them of a giraffe when he got in a hurry, rambling along as though the screws were loose in all his joints.

"You look comfortable," he said, glancing at her outfit.

She lounged on the porch steps, wearing overall shorts and a white T-shirt, with her bare feet stretched out in front of her. She wiggled her toes contentedly.

"Yeah," she smiled lazily. "Life is good."

He handed her a white sack with a bookstore logo on the front. "For you."

"Will, how sweet," she smiled warmly at him as she plunged into the sack and removed a book of poems by a favorite author. "You remembered I like poetry?"

He nodded. "So do I."

As Laurel looked up at Will, she saw a familiar expression in his eyes. She was not being conceited, merely honest, when she suspected Granny was right about his feelings for her.

"Here." She lifted the plate of cookies nestled beside her. "Get a handful. You could use a few more calories."

"You and your grandmother!" he said, shaking his head while reaching for a cookie. "Why isn't everyone fat?"

"I told you, we get our exercise clogging!"

He nodded. "Wish I could stay awhile."

Laurel munched a cookie and squinted at him through the sunlight. "Will, would you mind meeting Anna Lee Wentworth, the girl I'm tutoring? She's interested in photography. In fact," she brushed cookie crumbs from the bib of her overalls, "she just might grow up to be as passionate about photography as you are."

He was leaning against the porch post, sampling the cookie. "Okay. When?"

Laurel thought about her lesson plans for the week. "Just fit us into your schedule; we're flexible."

Will reached for another cookie. "I'll let you know."

"Fine. When are you going to Cades Cove?"

"I'll be going every day; I'll probably stay over there once I start work so I can capture sunrise and sunset. But I want to rest up for another week. This is the first vacation I've had in years."

Laurel reached out and yanked his sleeve. "Then take a load off your feet and sit down. Listen, Will, you need to learn to smell the roses. I think you're pushing yourself too hard."

Her tugging had yanked him down, very close beside her, and they both laughed. Suddenly he was serious again.

"You like Matt, don't you?"

She took a deep breath, thinking about her response.

"He *likes* you, you know. I sensed it when we were introduced at Pigeon Forge. So how do you feel about him?"

Laurel turned and looked at Will, seeing in his gray eyes the vulnerability that had always been there, emphasized even more by his plain features and long face.

"I don't know," she replied, looking away.

"Lau-rel. You're talking to Will, who knows that you bat your eyelashes when you try to lie."

"I do not!" She swatted at his shoulder, laughing, then looked away. "Yes, I do like him, unfortunately."

"Maybe it's more than *like?*"

She propped her elbows on the porch and leaned back, her head nestled against her shoulder.

"It won't do any good, Will. Even if he likes me a little, we don't have a chance."

"Because of his money?"

"Because his work is in Atlanta; my work is here. Right now, I don't feel like there is anything or anyone who could drag me out of these mountains. I don't belong in Atlanta."

"And Wentworth probably doesn't belong here."

"You got it," she said, her eyes still closed, her heart wrenching at the sad truth.

Silence stretched between them for several seconds.

"I almost fell in love with a secretary in my publisher's office," he said, after a thoughtful pause. "Almost. Then I got smart and realized we had absolutely nothing in common and never would."

187

Laurel opened her eyes and rolled her head on her shoulder to look at him. "Do you believe that, Will? I mean, you don't go with the old adage of love conquering all?"

He laughed, but it wasn't really a laugh, Laurel decided, more a sound of mockery.

"Nothing has ever been conquered for me by love. Hard work and determination, that's what conquers." Bitterness dripped from his voice as ne spoke, and Laurel was troubled to glimpse the sadness that seemed to weight his soul.

"Be right back," she said, getting up from the steps and hurrying inside. From the desk drawer she retrieved a small leather-bound New Testament. Each year when students left her class, it was her parting gift. This time, she'd ended up with an extra one from ordering an even two dozen.

She stepped back out on the porch, holding it behind her back. "You brought me a book. Now I have one for you." She saw his cynical expression as she handed it to him.

"I know you don't want it," she said, "but I want you to have it. And as a favor to Granny and me, I demand that you read a chapter every night until it's finished. Then I will personally come to New York and give you a quiz on what you've read."

He grinned. "Laurel, you and Granny still live in your own little world up here, don't you?"

She tilted her head to one side, regarding him solemnly. "And just what does living here have to do with my giving you a gift?"

He avoided the question, looking out at the street. "I remember you guys dragging me to a revival where the preacher hollered and pounded. That's not my style, Laurel. Sorry."

"It doesn't have to be. He was just giving his interpretation of what he'd read. You're free to make your own. Just give it a try; I think you'll be amazed at what can happen."

Since he hadn't accepted her gift, she leaned down and dropped it in his shirt pocket.

"I'd better get going," he said, coming to his feet.

"Don't let me run you off with my preaching and pounding!"

He grinned. "I know you mean well. Actually, I'd planned to visit a few friends in the area."

"Good idea. Listen, Will, Jessica Thorne is getting married this weekend, and I'm a bridesmaid. Why don't you come with me?"

"To a wedding? You know me better than that."

She nodded slowly. "Yeah, I guess I do."

"See you later," Will said, looking a bit sad.

Laurel suspected he was disappointed to learn of her feelings for Matt; unfortunately, there didn't seem to be anything she could do about her stubborn heart.

"Bye, Will." She smiled, watching him walk back to his car. Then she went back inside and tried to work up some enthusiasm for Jessica's wedding.

As soon as Laurel saw Jessica, she forgot her troubles of the past week.

"Laurel!" Jessica left her fiancé on the steps of the church and ran to hug her friend. It was almost time for the rehearsal, but the two girls were oblivious to everything as they hugged and talked at the same time.

"Jessica, you look wonderful," Laurel said, stepping back to look at her.

In contrast to Laurel's blonde beauty, Jessica had dark hair and eyes and the lean willowy body of a fashion model.

"Blake," Jessica swung around, motioning to him.

Blake Vandercamp was of medium build with dark hair and gray eyes. He wore expensive clothes and sported a healthy tan.

"So this is the third wallflower!" he teased.

Laurel burst into laughter. "You've obviously told him a few stories," she said.

"Come on," Fanny yelled from the church door, "we have a rehearsal to do."

Arm in arm, Laurel and Jessica entered the church. Laurel tried not to think about how she would feel if this were her rehearsal or her wedding that was planned for the next day.

After a few blunders, a difference of opinion between Jessica and Fanny, and a whispered joke among the groomsmen, the rehearsal finally ended, and everyone seemed relieved.

The wedding party piled into cars and drove to Pigeon Forge to have dinner. Laurel insisted on taking her own car, and over dinner, Jim and Rosemary and Laurel made plans for a reunion at Seascape, Jessica and Blake's new inn in Florida.

It was almost 1:00 A.M. when Laurel said goodnight and drove home, feeling more lonely that she had ever felt in her life. When she opened the screen to unlock the door, an envelope toppled onto the porch. Puzzled, she leaned down to pick it up, reading first her name, then spotting the Wentworth logo on the return address. Her heart beat faster as she hurried inside, flipping on lights as she ripped open the envelope.

She took a deep breath and read the short note.

Dear Laurel,

I flew back with Mother and Anna Lee today. Sorry I missed seeing you, but I have to return with the plane tonight. I'm sorry that we seem to be at odds on so many things. Perhaps when I come back we can talk.

Matt

She stared sadly at his name, wishing it could have read *Love, Matt.* Sighing, she folded the letter and returned it to the envelope. What was there to talk about? She found herself hoping once again that things were different, that Matt, instead of Will, had grown up here in the valley. But of course that was a ridiculous thing to wish, a silly fantasy.

She leaned her head against the back of the chair and closed her eyes. She had to accept reality. And Matthew Wentworth was merely a fantasy.

The wedding was sweet and sentimental, and everything went as planned. When Laurel returned home the next evening, she had just inserted her key in the lock when the phone rang. Trying to balance the load in her arms, she pushed the door open and fumbled for the light switch. Just as she lifted the receiver with hello forming on her lips, the line clicked.

She stood in the darkness, staring at the phone, somehow certain it was Matt.

You're overreacting from a romantic day, she scolded herself, trudging to her bedroom. When she met her reflection in the mirror, she stopped to stare. Tiny bits of rice still clung to her hair, and in her arms were her dulcimer, purse, and the bouquet she had caught from the bride. Her eyes lingered on the delicate sweetheart roses and baby's breath in the bridal bouquet.

Will it ever happen to me?

On Monday as Laurel drove up to the Wentworth house, she felt her muscles stiffen as her car topped the hill. She searched the driveway anxiously, knowing he would not be there. So why was she hoping? *Well, perhaps Anna Lee and I can get back to work with no interruptions.*

After Lou admitted Laurel, she entered the living room and found Anna Lee, slumped on the sofa, looking exhausted after her trip.

"Hi, I missed you," Laurel said genuinely.

"I missed you, too," Anna Lee replied. She glanced over her shoulder, lowering her voice. "While we were there, Mother told one of her friends that she hates it up here, and that we'll be returning to Atlanta soon." Her eyes were bleak as she stared into Laurel's face.

"Well, then we'll have to get busy so you'll be all set for eighth grade." She looked at the coral slacks and matching shirt Anna Lee was wearing.

"Anna Lee, you've lost some more weight," Laurel said tactfully. "I can tell."

Anna Lee peered at her from lowered eyebrows. "You can tell, really?"

"I certainly can."

"Matt brought up a special machine from Atlanta," she replied shyly. "It's upstairs. But I hate it."

Laurel reached over and squeezed Anna Lee's hand.

"But you're using it to work on your weight! I'm proud of you," she smiled into the girl's dreary face. "More importantly, don't you feel proud? You're doing something for yourself that no one else can do for you. That's a good feeling, don't you think?"

The expression of weariness slipped from Anna Lee's face as she pondered Laurel's words. "I guess so. It's a treadmill," she added, saying the word as though it were some horrible, unspeakable piece of torture.

"Are you sore from using it?" Laurel asked.

"I can hardly walk at all now," she said. Slowly a grin formed on her lips and her eyes danced with humor.

"But just think how healthy you'll be, and you'll have all new clothes when you start school this fall."

She shrugged. "I get new clothes every year anyway."

"Maybe this year, buying clothes will be more fun."

Anna Lee stared at her, obviously finding some comfort in that. Then her eyes brightened. "I'm going to tell Mother that I'm picking out my own stuff this year."

"Good. Hey, it's time to get to work," Laurel said. "But first, I brought those verses I told you about." She opened her notebook and removed the page she had tucked in it that morning. For a fraction of a second, her hand hesitated, clutching the verses. She found that sentimentally, she was reluctant to part with them. But then she looked back at Anna Lee and saw someone far more in need of inspiration than herself. And besides, she'd long since marked them in her Bible and committed them to memory.

Anna Lee took the soft, worn note paper, looking slightly embarrassed. "If you ever want this back..."

"No, those verses are filed in my head," Laurel smiled. "I memorized each of them. Now," she reached for a history book, "lets get to work."

"Wait! I forgot! I want to show you something."

Anna Lee grabbed Laurel by the arm and hauled her off the sofa. She didn't let up until they had gone through the kitchen and down the back steps to the patio. There was the puppy, her copper fur gleaming in the sunlight. A long leash stretched from her new collar up to a wire that extended from one tree to another, and she was happily trotting up and down the length of the line.

"Look! Isn't she beautiful!"

"Hi, Penny!" Laurel exclaimed, before she could catch herself.

Anna Lee turned. "How did you know her name?"

Laurel hesitated, searching frantically for a way to answer that question without telling a lie.

"Because you were here while we were away, weren't you?" Madeline spoke from behind them. She had been kneeling, inspecting a huge fern in a potted planter at the side of the patio.

Rather than looking refreshed after her trip to Atlanta, Madeline looked much worse in Laurel's opinion. Her eyes were dark-circled, and there was something odd about her stare. Laurel considered Madeline's snide insinuation and looked her squarely in the eye.

"Mrs. Wentworth, I stopped by to speak to your son about a community project."

Madeline glared at her, saying nothing, swaying a bit before she gripped the back of a chair.

"Come on, Penny!" Anna Lee had lost interest in the conversation as she turned back to the dog, snapping her fingers at her, laughing at her antics.

Laurel tried to think what else she could say to convince Madeline as the woman's eyes swept over her coldly.

"You came here to discuss a," her lips twisted around the words, "a community project with my son?"

Laurel could see Madeline thought she had some ulterior motive and was sneaking around her back to see Matt. She decided to explain exactly the way it had happened.

"He was washing the puppy out back here. I drove up and he came around the corner of the house and we spoke; then he showed me the dog and I left."

"I see," she said, her tone condescending. "In the future, I would prefer that you not come here when we're gone."

"Mother, why are you being so mean to Laurel?" Anna Lee thundered back, her hands on her hips, the puppy forgotten.

"I'm not being mean." Madeline flicked a minuscule piece of lint from her silk caftan. "It's just that I don't like having company here when I'm away." She looked at Anna Lee with a tight smile. "Sometimes we leave things in a mess, you know, and it's just embarrassing for guests to see."

Laurel glanced at Anna Lee, wondering if she believed that. "Anna Lee, shall we get back to work?" Laurel asked.

Anna Lee sulked, saying nothing more as she glanced back at the puppy and trudged inside with Laurel.

"Remember last week when I mentioned my friend Will, the photographer?" Laurel asked, trying to put the unpleasant scene behind them as they entered the living room again. "Well, he's home now, and I've told him about your interest in photography. He'd like to meet you."

Anna Lee came back to life. "Really? When?"

"Is Wednesday morning okay? That's when he said he could come over. I'll ask him to look at your camera and give you some tips."

For a moment, Anna Lee looked crestfallen. "Mother didn't take me shopping for a new camera and supplies like she promised. She got busy with her friends."

Laurel tried to suppress her annoyance with Madeline for breaking another promise. The more she knew about the woman, the more she disliked her.

"Perhaps Will can give you a tip on the best camera to purchase, since you haven't already done that. Now, shall we get to work?"

Anna Lee looked pleased as they settled down to the books, and the day passed swiftly.

On Tuesday, just before lunch was served, Matt wandered through the living room, taking them both by surprise.

"Hello," Laurel said, trying to force a smile.

"Hi."

"What are you doing back so soon?" Anna Lee demanded.

"We finally closed that deal I've been working on. Now I have business here," he said, and then headed toward the kitchen.

Laurel wondered about the nature of his business, while she tried to resume her little speech to Anna Lee about Sherman's march on Atlanta. The last thing on her mind, however, was history. She had already thought up her excuse when Lou called them to lunch. There was no way she could sit down to the table with both Madeline and Matt and not choke to death on her food.

"Anna Lee, I have to go to the dentist over our lunch hour. I'll be back at one. Is that okay with you?"

"Sure," she shrugged.

Laurel was out the door to her car before anyone could ask questions. She drove straight to Dr. Wallace's office, went in and made an appointment for the following week.

There, she thought smugly, *I've done something I needed to do while avoiding an unpleasant situation.* To kill more time, she stopped in at the post office to see if she had any mail.

Millie handed her a letter from her mother, then looked at her with wide curious eyes. "Have you heard?"

"I doubt it," Laurel said wearily, dreading the latest report on Cheryl and Matt.

"Two of the merchants from Pigeon Forge are meeting with the town council at the mayor's office."

"For what?" she asked distractedly, relieved that the news did not concern her or Matt. But she was wrong.

"There's a rumor buzzing that your friend is going to put in an outlet mall here."

"What friend?" Laurel asked, dropping her letter.

"Matt Wentworth."

Laurel knelt to pick up the envelope. "They're mistaken," she said weakly. "He'd never do that. He knows that we don't want our community to become another tourist trap."

Millie sniffed. "Apparently not everyone feels that way. There are a couple of merchants—I'll not name names—whose businesses are about to go under anyway. They think they can hop on the bandwagon and make a killing in the outlet business."

For a moment Laurel thought her knees were going to buckle. She leaned over the counter, staring into Millie's smug face. "Millie, surely you're mistaken," she said, her eyes begging Millie to retract what she had said, to laugh and confess that she was making a terrible joke.

As Millie looked at her, hesitating, Laurel thought, *Please, just once, be wrong about your information.*

"Sorry, I'm afraid it's true. Maybe you should ask him yourself," she inclined her head toward the highway as Matt's black Jeep zipped past.

"I will," Laurel said, rushing out the door.

Between the post office and the parking meter in front of the mayor's office, her mind neatly tallied up the facts to support Millie's gossip: Matt and Cheryl had been looking around in Pigeon Forge; he had been meeting with the mayor; the "new project" he had mentioned; even the look of regret on his face when he had said, on Saturday, that he wanted to explain something to her. But then he'd been in such a rush to get to Cheryl that he hadn't time to explain whatever was on his mind.

Well, there will never be enough time to explain the very project he knows I would oppose more than anything in the world. Angel Valley, an outlet center! The bumper to bumper traffic, the tourists, the car horns and strange faces, and the little park trampled and overrun. She hit the brakes too hard as she screeched to a stop at the parking meter. At least she caught his attention. He was already to the front door of the small building, his hand outstretched to open it, when he saw her.

His hand dropped to his side as his eyes met hers for a

moment. She whipped her lithe body out of the car, slamming the door behind her, and marched toward him. He broke the distance between them in a few long strides.

"Please tell me you're not involved in a plan to put an outlet center here," she said as he approached her.

As she spoke, her eyes dropped to his other hand, and she spotted the file folder. She suspected her question had just been answered.

"Laurel, why don't you come to this meeting? Hear what just a few outlets could do for industry?"

"Not to mention what it could do for your billfold! How could you?" she cried. "Our little community is the most beautiful, most unspoiled place in the world, but you just can't leave that alone, can you?"

"And you can't bear to share it with anyone," he retorted. "Don't you think you're being selfish? You have a good job with health insurance and benefits; you're forgetting others here who don't have health insurance because they can't afford it. Believe it or not, there are people who can foresee a way of doing things moderately without ruining your community!"

"You know very well there is no such thing as moderation when it comes to outlet malls and tourists. You saw that when you and Cheryl checked out Pigeon Forge! So drop your noble, caring act with me. You don't care about this place, or the people in it; all you care about is the money you'll make."

From the corner of her eye, she could see shopkeepers standing in doorways, and a few passersby stopping to gawk. She didn't care. She had never, in her entire life, been so angry or felt so used.

"Granny's land would have been just perfect for your little

project, wouldn't it? Right there on the highway, easy access, inexpensive to develop."

Matt's face darkened with fury as whispers flew over the crowd.

"Well, don't let me keep you," she said, fighting the tears. "You've already wasted too many valuable business hours on me, trying to get Granny's property, which would have been the best location anywhere. I think it's despicable," her eyes blazed fire into his face, "that you tried to take advantage of a vulnerable little widow who was kind to you."

"That's the worst thing anyone has ever said to me."

She stepped back from him, nodding slowly. "The truth hurts, doesn't it?"

She whirled and ran back to her car, jumped in, cranked up and drove off, barely missing Ol' Major as she careened around the curve. The men came up off their seats at the service station, staring openmouthed as she aimed her car toward her house and pressed the accelerator to the floorboard.

When she turned onto Elm and screeched into her driveway, she heard his siren hot on her trail.

Tears streamed down her face as she got out of the car and slammed the door with a fury.

Jasper lurched to a halt, bolting out of the car.

"Write me up, Jasper," she cried out before he could open his mouth. "I don't care. This little town is going to need all the fines you can dish out in the name of big business. In fact, you're going to be very, very busy, Jasper. You'll be handing out tickets every day, dozens of them," Laurel yelled, sobbing openly. "And you'll need a partner, a new patrol car, maybe even a new jail."

Jasper's eyes practically bulged from their sockets.

"I'm not writing you a ticket, Laurel; we're calling an ambulance. You've lost it!"

Thirteen

The last time Laurel had been forced to go to bed, blinds drawn, phone off the hook, utterly devastated, was after the death of her father. Of course, no pain could be as severe as the death of her father, at least none that she could imagine. Yet she felt as though there had been another kind of death.

The death of trust. And with that pain came a cold hard assurance that she would never again care for another man. She simply could not risk her judgment. *Look where it's gotten me—first Ryan Thompson and now Matt Wentworth, who is far more dangerous than Ryan.* For she had fallen head over heels with Matt, and only now could she begin to assess the damage.

She called Anna Lee, saying she was sick and couldn't come back for the afternoon. Her heart was a stone in her chest; her throat was dry from rasping sobs. Even Granny was unable to comfort her and finally went home, feeling a bit disillusioned herself. Granny called back later with the news that Matt had phoned her and assured her that he had not tried to purchase her land for an outlet; that he hadn't even thought of it at the time. Laurel, however, closed her ears to anything more, refusing to listen to the words he had used to deceive Granny.

Darkness settled over her lonely little house. Down the street somewhere she could hear the Bailey twins out on their skateboards in the middle of the street. And she thought she could smell charcoal smoke from someone's backyard barbecue. It would all change, end. Nothing in Angel Valley would ever be the same again, but she was powerless to stop it. The Wentworths were too important, too wealthy.

Laurel dragged herself up out of bed, oblivious to her wrinkled clothes, and padded to the kitchen, hitting the light switch by the door. She hadn't eaten a bite since breakfast, which consisted of two pieces of toast and a glass of orange juice. She wandered to the refrigerator to survey her choices, but as her swollen eyes squinted down into the meager contents, she let the door swing shut. She simply couldn't force a bit down her throat, raw from rasping sobs.

Grabbing the tea kettle, she sloshed it once to be sure there was water, then turned on the burner. Opening the small canister of tea bags, she dropped one into a cup and stared dully at the kettle, waiting for the steam to rise.

The phone rang again, but she ignored it. Finally, the reality of her shouting match in front of the mayor's office hit her. She felt like a fool. She still didn't regret her words, she just hoped that her students' parents, former or future, wouldn't think she was a closet maniac.

She sighed, closing her eyes as she leaned against the cabinet, willing the phone to stop. Finally, it did. *What am I going to do?* This was her home, but perhaps he had been right. She was being selfish. *If the people really want industry, let them have it.* But she'd move somewhere else. The thought of leaving Angel Valley was like a spear in her heart. She had tried living elsewhere and hated every minute of it.

The kettle sang, and she opened her eyes, staring at the rising steam. Reaching for a potholder, she gripped the handle of the kettle, tilted the spout, and stared glumly at the hot water flowing over her tea bag.

If only there was a way she could pour peace over her tortured soul. As suddenly as the thought came to her, the answer was provided as well. She set the kettle down and picked up her tea cup, wandering to the table. She turned the globe on over her kitchen table. Her Bible lay open from that morning, where she had read her devotion and then removed the page of verses she had taken to Anna Lee.

"God, you've given me a real mountain this time," she said, staring at the Bible. "I just don't think I can climb it on my own. You'll have to show me the way. . .and give me the strength."

She set her tea cup down and gently pulled the Bible in front of her. With tender fingers, she smoothed out the page and read.

The next morning Laurel dressed with care. Neat black linen slacks, a ruffled white blouse, pearl studs in her ears. She brushed her blonde hair about her face until it shone with golden brilliance. She added extra blush to offset her pale skin and applied another coat of mascara to make up for the puffy eyes. Then she thrust her black-stocking feet into a pair of Italian loafers—last year's Christmas present from her mom—and turned off the light in the bedroom.

Gathering up her books and purse, she wondered how she had the nerve to show her face at the Wentworth house. But as she locked the door and headed to her car, she thought of something. If Madeline had heard of the scene in town, she would probably be relieved, even pleased. For now there was no chance of the little mountaineer and her shrewd son ever getting together.

"Yep, Madeline must be purring now," she said, cranking the engine and backing out of the driveway.

Reaching for her sunglasses to offset the sun's glare, she took a long, deep breath. It was amazing, but for some strange reason she found new strength seeping through her and wondered, after a sleepless night, from where it had come. Slowly her eyes lifted toward the heavens and she smiled. *Silly question.*

To her enormous relief, Matt's Jeep was not in the drive. Anna Lee informed her, soon after she arrived, that Matt had returned to Atlanta. Laurel eased into the morning without a glimpse of Madeline or a hint that anything had gone wrong the day before. She and Anna Lee spent a quiet day going over new material in her books and Madeline was not present for their fruit salad when Lou announced lunch.

As Laurel took her seat at the dining room table, she faced the glass wall, overlooking the patio. Her eyes lingered on the wicker table and chairs, and the memory of that hour she had spent with Matt returned to haunt her. She turned back to her plate, trying desperately to shut out the memory of his kiss. She thought she had until Anna Lee spoke up.

"What's wrong with your eyes?" she asked curiously.

"What do you mean?"

"It looks like you're crying."

Laurel dabbed a napkin to her lashes, then regretted the smudge of mascara on the crisp linen.

"An allergy," she said, picking up a plump red grape and popping it into her mouth.

"Can we go out and play with the puppy after we eat?" Anna Lee asked eagerly.

"No, I don't think so. Sorry, Anna Lee, but we have a lot of material to cover if we're going to spend tomorrow at the library."

"You said Will was coming over in the morning," Anna Lee said. Already her round face was taking on that look of despair, and Laurel could only imagine how many times promises to her had been broken.

"Yes, he is. We're going to the library afterward."

"Oh." Anna Lee said.

Laurel survived the afternoon by reminding herself that she and Anna Lee would be out of the house most of the following day. She planned to find every excuse possible to be gone, hoping to avoid Madeline and Matt, in case he returned.

As Laurel left for the day, Anna Lee chattered about her photograph album and her camera and film, all of which she planned to show Will.

She looked at Anna Lee and tried to smile. It was good to see her looking happy, while Laurel struggled with depression. It was as though they had switched temperaments.

Laurel drove home and deliberately bypassed the post office. She couldn't bear to face Millie, for she suspected today's hot news was Laurel's temper tantrum in front of the mayor's office.

She sighed heavily, hoping somehow she would learn a valuable lesson through all of the disappointment.

Fourteen

❧

G ranny called Laurel at six in the morning, asking her to come by for coffee before going to the Wentworth house.

"Can't it wait?" Laurel asked crossly, rubbing the sleep from her eyes.

"Nope."

Laurel showered and dressed quickly then drove to her grandmother's house, wondering what was up.

She arrived to find Granny and Will at the kitchen table, lounging over coffee and biscuits.

"Pull up a chair," Granny called pleasantly. "You look like you need one of my biscuits with a heavy dose of gravy."

Laurel took a look at Will's plate, filled to overflowing, and felt sick. "There's no way I can eat a big breakfast," she said, sinking into a chair. "What's up?"

Granny handed her a cup of coffee, then placed a fluffy biscuit before her.

"My phone hasn't stopped ringing," she said.

"Neither has mine."

"Then why didn't you answer it?" Granny snapped.

Laurel sighed. "I've made a fool of myself, Granny."

Will's hand covered hers, and she turned and looked into kind gray eyes. "No, you haven't. You've stood up for the right thing, which is more than a lot of other people have the guts to do!"

"Thanks, Will." She smiled at him.

He had always been so kind to her. Why couldn't she fall in love with Will? He was a good person who always seemed to understand her feelings.

Granny took a seat and folded her hands on the table.

"Young lady, you've caused quite a stir."

Laurel leaned back in the chair and heaved a sigh. "Granny, if you've called me over here to fuss at me, I want you to know, I'm not up to it."

"I'm not about to fuss at you," she said gently, patting her arm. "I just thought you might like to know what happened after you put Matt Wentworth in his place."

Laurel held her breath, afraid to ask.

"I heard from Harold, who's on the town council, that the mayor had just about persuaded the council members to agree to a small outlet center."

"It won't stay small," Laurel cried.

"Let me finish, please. They were all seated around the conference table, waiting for Matt. Then, after you two had words, he walked into the meeting and said he was retracting his proposal for the outlets. That's right," she emphasized, as Laurel's mouth fell open. "There will be no outlets here. As for those needing work and health insurance, he's going to put them on the company payroll and find something for them to do right here at home."

Laurel stared at her grandmother. "How is he going to do that?"

"He's going to build a community hall with an art center. Locals who do arts and crafts and need a place to work or to store their goods will do so in the hall. Clarence will oversee the operation, and there'll be a big truck with drivers hired to deliver our products for consignment to shops across the country." Her eyes twinkled. "That will keep America out of Angel Valley!"

Laurel was speechless and could only stare wide-eyed at her grandmother. It was almost more than she could comprehend, and she felt certain the town must be agog. No wonder her phone was ringing off the hook.

"When did he think of all that?" she finally asked.

"Apparently, he had already been thinking about a community hall, along with the outlet thing. Once you had your say, I guess everything came together in his mind." Granny sighed. "It was a very noble and generous thing for him to do. You just might tell him so today."

Laurel shook her head. "I can't. He's gone back to Atlanta."

"Well, I dare say he'll be coming again."

"Not to see me," she said, fighting tears. "Not after all the things I said to him."

"True love finds a way," Granny assured her.

Will cleared his throat. "Laurel, do you still want me to meet the Wentworth girl this morning?"

Laurel nodded. How on earth was she going to be a teacher today? It was impossible.

"My ulcer is acting up," she said, pressing a hand to her stomach.

"Will, why don't you go on over to the Wentworth house?" Granny suggested. "It's almost 8:00. Laurel needs to calm herself before she tries to deal with the Wentworth females!"

Will looked out at the sky. "I have an idea, Laurel. It's a beautiful day; I can give Anna Lee some pointers on taking pictures. I'll drive over and pick her up and you can meet us in the park."

"A photography class," she nodded. "Perfect. Will, I don't know how to thank you."

"You already have. I can never repay all the kindnesses you and Granny have shown me through the years. Don't worry about a thing. Just meet us in the park around nine."

Laurel tried to smile, while holding her stomach. The pain just grew worse. Granny scurried around, finding stomach medicine for Laurel before warming some milk. Within the hour, Laurel felt better. After touching up her makeup, she reached out to Granny, giving her a hug.

"Honey, everything will be all right," Granny smiled into her eyes. "After all, that man is in love with you."

"I don't know," Laurel replied, still doubtful. *In love with her? Was it possible?* Her mind drifted back to the time they had spent together. The look in his eyes, the words he had spoken to her, the kisses. Could it be true? If he had been someone other than Matt Wentworth, she would have believed that he loved her. *But then,* she drew a deep ragged breath, *if he was someone else, she might not love him.* It wasn't the money or the status, it was Matt. She loved everything about him until yesterday when she had thought the worst of him and went into a blind rage.

"Don't be too hard on yourself," Granny said, patting Laurel's cheek. "You spoke up for your beliefs, which is exactly what your parents taught you to do. I'm glad they succeeded." She smiled adoringly at her granddaughter.

Laurel swallowed around the lump in her throat. "I love you," she said, as they hugged again before she hurried out the door.

Laurel parked on the east side of the park and walked toward the bench where Ol' Major lay. It was a gorgeous July morning, and as she looked around the quaint little town, hearing only the sounds of birdsong and an occasional car, she suddenly was very clear about who she was and how she felt.

She settled onto a wrought-iron bench and leaned down to stroke Ol' Major's sleepy face.

The one thing she would have liked to change was her attack on Matt. She had said some horrible things to him. She owed him an apology, particularly since he had gone out of his way to try to do something for the people here.

She lifted her eyes from Ol' Major's sleepy face and glanced around her. Merchants were sweeping off their front sidewalks and watering the geraniums in their flower boxes. She closed her eyes, sniffing the smells of Angel Valley as she thanked God for allowing her to live here, to be who she was.

Hearing the roar of Will's sports car, she opened her eyes and peered toward the curb.

Through the windshield of the car, Laurel spotted Anna Lee hugging the door. Even at a distance, Laurel could see that Anna Lee's cheeks were glowing and her eyes were smiling. Laurel felt sure she'd never had an experience quite like this one.

She waved to Anna Lee, who waved back before she turned, fumbling with the door handle.

Laurel walked over to the car, smiling at Will.

"Thanks, Will," she said to him as he got out and stretched his legs. He wore faded jeans and a well-worn T-shirt. Laurel couldn't help wondering why he had chosen this day to wear his old clothes, but that was Will. Always doing things his own way.

"You're welcome," he said, reaching into the back seat for his camera case. Anna Lee, with her camera strapped around her neck, walked quickly in Laurel's direction.

"Hi there," Laurel smiled at her. "What do you think of photography 101? Does it suit you?"

Anna Lee glanced shyly at Will, locking his car.

"This will be neat!" Anna Lee said, grinning from ear to ear.

"Another new outfit?" Laurel smiled at the denim jumpsuit.

"Yes. Do you like it?"

"I like it a lot. And you really are making progress," she said under her breath, not wanting to embarrass Anna Lee with Will only a few steps away.

"Anna Lee," Laurel hesitated, choosing her words, "was it all right with your mother for you to come to the park?"

Anna Lee shrugged. "I guess so. She'd gone to get her medicine refilled. I left a note...," her words trailed as she stared into space.

"What's wrong?" Laurel asked.

Will joined them, surveying the park appreciatively while removing his camera from the case. "Ol' Major would be a perfect subject," he said.

"I wrote the note in my tablet, but I forgot to tear it out. The phone rang and...,"

Her words were interrupted by the screech of brakes. Madeline's Mercedes careened to a stop in the center of the street. The driver's door flew open and Madeline leaped out, her eyes wild.

"Anna Lee!" she screamed, running toward the park.

Anna Lee froze in her tracks, startled by her mother's odd behavior.

A siren sounded as Jasper roared up behind her, blue light flashing.

"There they are," Madeline called to Jasper as he jumped from his vehicle. Madeline ran toward the park, almost tripping on the curb in her desperate flight to reach her daughter.

"Anna Lee, come here!"

Startled, the girl hurried to her mother's side, and Madeline began to sob hysterically. Her face was chalk white as she clutched Anna Lee against her.

Laurel approached slowly, realizing Madeline had not found the note. But she had mentioned it to her at the dining room table last week, hadn't she? She frowned. No, she hadn't. Will hesitated in the background, uncertain of what to do.

"Are you all right?" Jasper was peering down at Anna Lee.

Madeline whirled around, looking from Jasper to Laurel, then Will. Suddenly, the fear that had contorted her features changed to something else: pure, unbridled rage. She whirled on Will.

"You tried to kidnap my daughter!" she glared at him. "Deputy, I demand that you arrest these two. That...that hippie abducted her from the house. And this woman masterminded their little scheme."

"Mother!" Anna Lee pulled back from her, horrified.

Laurel had reached Madeline by now, and while her words—and their obvious implication—stung to the core, her first reaction was to try and calm Madeline.

"Mrs. Wentworth, we were going to take some pictures here in the park and—"

"I don't believe you!" Madeline snapped. She trembled, and her eyes were wild in her ghostly face. "You've done nothing but disrupt my family ever since you came. As for him," she looked at Will, "he obviously hasn't a dime to his name. I know exactly why he took Anna Lee from the house."

"Mother, stop it!" Anna Lee cried, trying to silence the woman's reckless words.

Jasper stepped between them now, aware he should be doing his duty, whatever it was.

"Laurel, what's going on?" he demanded, his tone sharper than necessary.

Three of the merchants were walking toward the park, their faces filled with concern. Even Ol' Major, disturbed by the loud voices, had come to his feet and ambled toward Billy, who looked confused and bewildered as he stood on the opposite street corner.

"I had asked Will to give Anna Lee a lesson in photography," Laurel said, trying to control the tremor in her voice. "Since I wasn't feeling well this morning, he offered to pick her up and meet me here at the park."

"Surely you don't believe a ridiculous story like that," Madeline retorted, glaring at Jasper. She gripped Anna Lee's wrist while the girl struggled to free herself. "My housekeeper said this man took her away without an explanation!"

Jasper gulped, appraising the situation. "Well, er, Mrs. Wentworth, if they were trying to kidnap her, as you reported, I don't think they'd be out here in the park where—"

"I should have known!" Madeline cried, overpowering Anna Lee and yanking her back to the car. "You'd defend them, of course." Her eyes blazed over the group that had gathered. "This is nothing but a redneck, hole-in-the-wall with a bunch of simpletons trying to run the place!"

Anna Lee's cheeks flamed and she began to sob, obviously humiliated beyond words as her mother dragged her to the car and shoved her into the front seat. Madeline flew around to the driver's side, then whirled, glaring back at Laurel and Will.

"I know what you were up to," she screamed. "And don't you ever come near us again!"

With that she leaped into the front seat and cranked the engine.

The big car roared to life and leaped forward, just as Ol' Major crossed the road, his sleepy eyes focused on Billy. If Madeline saw him, she never attempted to slow down. The front bumper caught him against the head with a terrible thud and the dog fell under the car.

Billy raced forward and fell to his knees, bursting into tears as he looked at the dog. Will rushed to Billy's side, trying to comfort him as the shopkeepers gathered, staring in horror from Billy and the dog, back to Laurel, as tears streamed down her cheeks.

She couldn't believe what she had witnessed. Had Madeline's mind snapped out of fear for her daughter, or had her drugs distorted everything, robbing her of sound judgment and common sense?

Fifteen

❦

W e're leaving!" Anna Lee's voice came over the telephone wire in a broken sob. Laurel frowned, gripping the phone tighter, staring blankly through her kitchen window to the twilight settling over her backyard.

"Now? You're going tonight?"

"Mother won't listen to anything," Anna Lee's voice broke as she tried to explain. "I told her about the note, but she paid no attention. She said I shouldn't try to protect you." A sob ripped through her words. "She's called the plane to come pick us up. We're leaving the car and most of our things. She said she'd send someone back to get everything. Laurel, I've never seen her act like this. And she takes pills all the time."

Laurel took a deep breath, trying to think of what to say. She couldn't encourage Anna Lee to disobey her mother, and yet the woman had ceased to be reasonable.

"Anna Lee, I think you should try and reach your brother; tell him what's going on. Maybe he can calm your mother down."

"I tried. Matt's not at the office or home. I don't know what else to do." She whispered into the phone. "I have to go. The plane is already here."

Anna Lee's sobs tore at Laurel's heart, and she wished desperately there was something she could do to help.

"Anna Lee, I'll see you again. I'll find a way," she promised, as the phone clicked in her ear.

She held the phone for several seconds, staring out at the growing darkness before she replaced the headset in its cradle on the kitchen wall. She thought about what Anna Lee had said about the pills and suspected that overmedication was part of Madeline's problem. What could she do?

She paced back and forth across the kitchen floor. Why had she promised Anna Lee she would see her again? When would she? How? Madeline would forbid Anna Lee to talk to her. It was too late to do anything; probably too late to make amends with Matt.

She walked into the living room and stared out into the growing darkness. The walls seemed to be closing in on her, and Laurel knew there was no way she could settle down to a magazine or a television program. She needed to jog the block, but that didn't seem to provide enough space either.

She picked up her purse and car keys and headed out the door. She was almost inside the car before she realized what was motivating her. Laurel's basic instinct was to head to the small airport in Sevierville, from which they would be leaving. Maybe she could see Anna Lee one more time, calm her down. She started the car and drove down Elm Street, staring into the darkness, her mind muddled with conflict.

She had to be reasonable. Even if she managed to get to the airport before the plane took off, what good would it do? In

Madeline's frame of mind, seeing Laurel would just make her more hysterical. She turned the corner onto Main, staring blankly past the frame houses where lights blinked in windows, a peaceful setting on a summer night. No, it wouldn't do any good to go to the airport. Madeline would forbid Anna Lee to see her.

Accept the truth, Laurel; they're gone, out of your life. Forever.

A low rumble of thunder growled through the night clouds as she drove toward her grandmother's house. Before reaching the driveway, however, she turned around. She didn't really want to face Will, not yet. She had apologized to him over and over. He seemed to be all right; still, she wondered if shy, gentle Will hadn't been more hurt by Madeline's remarks than he would admit.

Granny would want to give her some advice, but Laurel wanted to work through this one alone. She drove past the school, dark except for the night lights, and forced herself to think of her other students, wonderful, appreciative students with kind, loving parents. Still, she could not keep Anna Lee from her thoughts; the pain in her voice haunted her like a nightmare.

She circled down Main Street where all was quiet except for the sheriff's office. Suddenly, the door flew open, and Jasper ran down the steps, hopping into his car. She slowed down, taking a deep breath. Apparently he had picked up something on the scanner and was out to save the town.

Brakes squealing, he sped out of the parking lot. Laurel drove slowly by, embarrassed to look at him again after the scene she had made in her driveway.

His horn blared behind her. She adjusted the rearview mirror and saw that he motioned her to pull over.

Now what? She eased her car over to the edge of the road and rolled down her window. *What was going on?*

He pulled in behind her, screeching to a stop. *What in the world was he up to now?* she wondered, as she watched his door fly open. Jasper leaped out, running up to her car.

"Do you know how to reach Matt Wentworth?" he asked.

Laurel stared for a second. "Yes, but—"

"May be a false alarm, but Robert Walker's usually right." Jasper's eyes were wide in his thin face.

Her mind raced ahead. Robert was a local farmer ten miles out of town.

"I don't understand—"

"Robert just called," Jasper explained breathlessly. "Said a small plane was in trouble on the back of his farm. Sheriff Conway phoned the airport. The Wentworth plane left at 8:15. Knoxville airport's not picking them up on radar. I'm headed to the Walkers' now."

"I'm coming too," Laurel said, trying to think what to do. "If I need to reach Matt, I can call him from Robert's farm."

Jasper jumped back in his patrol car and burned rubber. Laurel pulled back onto the road to follow, her thoughts whirling like the blue light on his patrol car. The Walker farm. The plane could hardly have gotten airborne, but then she had heard many accidents occurred upon takeoff or soon afterward.

The rain fell harder. Diving into her purse for her glasses and clamping them on, she told herself she had to be careful and calm. Keeping Jasper's taillights in her vision, she prayed. Desperately.

God, protect them. Please, please...

The windshield wipers swished back and forth across the grimy windshield, an accompaniment to her urgent prayer.

As soon as she turned the curve, she saw the farmhouse blazing with lights; in addition to the Walker truck and car, two four-wheel-drive vehicles were parked in the drive. Jasper had just arrived and joined a group of men clustered together in the driveway. Through the misting rain, everyone stood with their heads tilted back, looking into the stormy sky just west of the house.

Her car lurched to a halt, and skidding a few feet in the process, attracted everyone's attention. She was too worried to be embarrassed as she hopped out of the car and ran up the driveway.

"Did the plane go down?" she called out.

Robert Walker was a typical Tennessee farmer: solid, competent, kind-spoken. His boots crunched over the wet gravel of the driveway as he hurried across to Laurel.

"I'm afraid so," he nodded. The gesture sent a rivulet of water from the wide brim of his rain hat. "We don't know for certain who it was."

Jasper spoke up. "The sheriff just radioed me. He's talked to the airport again. According to the flight plan filed by Wentworth's pilot, ten minutes from the airport would put them right about over your place, Robert."

There was a moment of silence as everyone digested this latest bit of news. Then Robert turned back to Laurel. "I heard a plane engine when I was out feeding the dogs, about half an hour ago; sounded like it was in trouble. I ran back up on the porch where I could see better. It was dropping lower and lower over the south end of my farm, over near the foothills." He paused, touching her arm. "Come on inside out of the rain."

She followed him to the back porch, nodding a greeting to Fats Watson and Clarence Adkins, whose farms adjoined the Walker farm.

"I heard the plane," Clarence was explaining to Jasper, "but Fats didn't. So it must be down in that stretch of woods between my place and his."

Jasper whirled, striding back to his car. "I'm gonna radio the sheriff. We'd better have a doctor ready."

His words sent Laurel's heart racing as she stepped into the warmth of Margaret Walker's kitchen. Clara Watson and Emily Adkins were seated at the kitchen table, drinking coffee. Running a hand over her tousled hair, Laurel turned to the women. "How did you get here so fast?"

Margaret Walker smiled at Laurel, and pressed a steaming mug of coffee into her hand.

"Robert called our house first," Clara explained to Laurel. "I was standing at the kitchen sink, washing dishes. I'd been hearing a funny sound, wasn't sure what it was. After Robert phoned, Fats ran outside and heard the engine, but we couldn't see the plane."

"And we never saw or heard it," Emily spoke up, "but Clarence wanted to come right over, see if we could help."

Margaret looked at Laurel with kind blue eyes that reflected her concern. "Is it the Wentworth plane?" she asked gently.

Margaret, like her husband, was a kind and caring person. She and Robert were parents to four children. Laurel had taught one of the younger ones, Paula, an adorable little girl with auburn curls and inquisitive blue eyes.

"I'm afraid so." She glanced at the women, who quietly sipped their coffee, and stared down at the table. Laurel wondered if they were thinking about Madeline Wentworth and the insulting words she had flung at the town.

Rednecks...living in a hole in the wall....

What else had she said? Laurel tried to remember, while her eyes roamed over the kitchen, seeking a telephone. She had to reach Matt to see if he had heard anything.

"Margaret, I need to make a phone call," she said.

Margaret nodded, leading her into a small den just off the kitchen. "Use that one. You'll have more privacy." She walked out, closing the door behind her.

Laurel hurried to the desk and sank, weak-kneed, into a chair. She ran a hand over her brow, trying to think. Matt had given her his telephone number, but of course the number was at home in her desk drawer. She'd try information, praying he didn't have an unlisted number.

To her surprise, she got the number quickly, and took a deep breath just before he answered on the second ring.

"Matt, this is Laurel." There was a momentary pause, but she plunged into the bad news, explaining everything she knew, then asking him if he could check with his office to see if there had been word from the plane.

"Perhaps it's just a false alarm," she finished shakily, using the words Jasper had spoken to her earlier.

"Give me that number," he said quickly. He spoke in a calm, controlled manner, yet she could hear the husky edge to his voice. "Thanks. I'll call back."

He hung up without a goodbye as Laurel took another deep

breath, trying to remain calm. She got up and returned to the kitchen, concentrating on positive thoughts.

"I'm surprised to see you here," Clara said, as Laurel took a seat at the table. "Fats came home and told us how that Wentworth woman talked to you today. She's terrible!"

"Don't know that I want Clarence out in the rain looking for her," Emily said. "If not for what the son is trying to do for everyone..."

Laurel nodded. "I know. Madeline Wentworth has some serious problems, but Anna Lee wants to do the right thing. And Matt...," she bit her lip.

Margaret pulled a pound cake from the oven and brought it to the table.

"No matter what any of you say," Margaret spoke calmly, "you know as well as I that we don't back off when somebody's in trouble. No matter who it is," she added quietly, glancing toward the window as a rumble of thunder shook the roof.

Laurel jumped at the sound and began to tremble. Clara laid a plump hand on her arm. "Drink your coffee, Laurel. And eat a slice of cake. You're pale as a ghost."

"I couldn't swallow a bite," she said, but she lifted the coffee mug to her mouth, needing the warmth and the caffeine.

She could hear more heavy-duty vehicles arriving. Margaret peered out the window. "Bobby Duke is here with his pick-up. If they have to go up the side of the mountain, he's got the best truck for it."

The phone rang, breaking the silence. Laurel had already put down her coffee and stood, waiting.

"It's for you," Margaret said. "Do you want to take it in—"

223

Laurel shook her head and grabbed the phone. It was Matt.

"Laurel, we can't make contact with the plane. The people I've spoken with are sure there's a problem. Nobody's picking them up on radar. They must be down."

The rain beat hard against the roof as another blast of thunder shook the rafters.

"I'm leaving in a few minutes," Matt said. "They're fueling the plane now."

"You aren't flying!" she blurted, then forced herself to speak in a more rational tone. "Should you...I mean...if the weather is bad...," her voice trailed. She couldn't bear to think of the same thing happening to Matt.

"The company has a bigger plane; I'll be safe, but we'll have to land in Knoxville. I'll decide when I get there whether to rent a car or chance a smaller plane the rest of the way."

"Matt, don't take chances. Please!"

He hesitated momentarily. "All right. I'll see you as soon as I can get there."

"Be careful," she pleaded again, then hung up the phone.

Tears were threatening, but she sank her teeth into her lower lip and fought for composure. *This is no time to lose it.* She had to keep a level head. She had to try and help, any way she could, and she would only be troublesome if she got hysterical. She walked to the table, sat down, and took a sip of coffee. Everyone had heard the conversation, but out of respect nobody said anything until she had a chance to settle her nerves.

The back door flew open and Robert poked his head in. "We're loading up in a couple of trucks and heading to the back side of the mountain."

"I want to go," Laurel came out of her chair so suddenly that she knocked her coffee over. One of the women quickly cleaned up the mess as Laurel rushed to Robert's side, tugging at his arm.

"Please, I just have to be there. Anna Lee will need me," she said. "And I promise not to be in the way."

"Laurel, the weather is getting worse," Robert answered. "And I don't know how long we'll be out there."

"I know, but I'd like to go. Surely there'll be something I can do to help."

"Let her go," Margaret said, pushing a slicker and gloves into Laurel's hands. "It can't hurt to have her along."

"Robert, can't you get an official rescue team out here? A chopper from Knoxville?" Emily asked, glancing worriedly out the window.

"The sheriff's already called. We're not sure the plane is down, and even so, it's too dangerous to send a chopper out right now. Paramedics are on the way, but if the people are trapped in the plane, hurt—" He cut his words off and turned for the door. "We have to go ourselves. Every minute is crucial if they're losing blood." He glanced back at Laurel as she shoved her arms into the sleeves of the slicker.

Laurel could see that Robert was still apprehensive, but at least he hadn't said no. Her thoughts flew in all directions as she tugged on the gloves. Robert was right; every moment was crucial. They couldn't wait for outside help; they had to do what they could this very minute.

She glanced back at the silent women. Every face was a picture of concern, yet none of them objected to their husbands' joining in the search. She called a goodbye over her shoulder as she left the house and scanned the vehicles.

225

Robert's red Ford Bronco was backed up to the porch, and the men were loading blankets and flashlights into the rear. Clarence and Fats were busy with their vehicles; one man was cleaning off his windshield, the other one was checking something under the hood of his truck.

Jasper's voice rang out over the group. "I've got my cellular phone. Bobby Duke and I will lead the way."

Laurel broke from the porch and sloshed across the yard to Bobby's truck, equipped with a roll bar and spotlights. If Jasper were traveling in the vehicle, it obviously had the best chance of reaching the terrain where the plane might have crashed. She could hear the men dividing up territories, calculating the quickest way to cover the land, as she reached the big truck.

Bits of conversation drifted to her.

"Depends on if they struck a tree going down...."

"...Don't see how he could land it in a safe place, once he got past the open fields. There's rocks and steep mountainside over there."

"...Hard to see."

Laurel bit her lip, closed her eyes, and prayed even harder as she reached for the door handle of Bobby's truck.

Jasper ran up, dripping with rain. "What do you think you're doing, Laurel?"

She sidestepped him and crawled into the cab of the truck. "I'm going along. There are two women in that plane—they'll need another woman."

Bobby Duke sat behind the wheel of his truck, revving the engine. As she settled into the seat beside him, he sidled a grin at her, as though they were loading up to chase deer.

"We'll lead the way," Jasper yelled to the others as he piled in on the passenger's side. He glanced at Laurel, shook his head, then motioned Bobby to go.

Bobby yanked the gear shift to low and the big truck leaped forward and hurtled toward the distant fields.

Laurel kept quiet as the big truck groaned up steep hills, then plunged into ravines. The torturous search seemed to go on for hours, with vehicles starting, stopping, radioing back and forth. The roads were slick with mud, and soon the windshield was a gray mess. At one point, the search party met up again, dispensing hot coffee, and speculated further on where to head next.

Robert Walker had an idea. "If the pilot veered off course for some reason, he would have gone toward that steepest drop-off." He pointed in the opposite direction from which they had been searching.

"We'll take a look," Jasper yelled, and everyone bolted back to their vehicles.

Laurel's heart was lodged in her throat as Bobby's truck moaned and groaned up the road that snaked the mountainside. She knew the drive was treacherous, and it amazed her that everyone was willing to risk their lives for people they didn't know.

She would have covered every stretch of ground by foot, if necessary, to try to find Anna Lee, the pilot, even Madeline. But she had a personal interest while—

"Hold it, Bobby!" Jasper yelled.

The truck lurched to a halt, and skidded. For a moment, Laurel thought they were going over. She bit her lips until she tasted blood.

"Shine your light down there." Jasper had rolled the window

down and thrust his head out in the rain, staring into the ravine on his side.

Bobby turned on the spotlight and Jasper began punching buttons on his phone.

"Can't get a frequency here." He barreled out of the truck and waved his flashlight over his head, back and forth. Farther down the mountain she could hear the other vehicles groaning up the steep road, then lurching to a stop as Jasper yelled to them.

"We've found them!" he yelled. "We've found them!"

$\mathscr{S}ixteen$

⚬⚬⚬

Outside the truck, the rain fell harder. Laurel peered through the gray mist out front, to the side, and in the back. The road made a hairpin curve, and she could see car lights of the other vehicles pinpointing the rainy darkness a quarter of a mile below. A car door slammed, and a voice echoed across the ravine. The other men jumped out of their vehicles, scrambling down the side of the mountain. Their flashlights threw tiny golden circles into the darkness.

Laurel got out of the truck, squinting through the rain. The pinpoints of light disappeared as the men descended into the ravine.

She couldn't bear to think how far down the plane had plunged or what it had struck along the way. The thought of Anna Lee and Madeline trapped way down there brought goose bumps over Laurel's skin, and terror gripped her as she pondered the possibilities. Could the Wentworths and the pilot have survived the crash? Were they alive now? And how on earth would these men be able to get them out?

Her knees trembled as she sank into the front seat of the truck. All she could do was pray.

By the clock, only ten minutes had passed when Bobby reappeared.

Laurel stuck her head out the window. "What's going on?"

"It's the plane, for sure." He went around the truck, checking each tire.

"What about the Wentworths?"

"Don't know. It's a mess down there. We won't know anything until we get inside the plane. And when we do, we gotta have paramedics and an ambulance."

As he spoke, she could hear an odd screeching sound coming from the ravine.

"What's that noise?" she asked as the rain peppered her face.

"The men brought tools. They're using a hacksaw and crowbar to try to pry open the door to the plane."

Removing his wet coat, he got in the truck and slammed the door. Laurel jumped, her nerves practically shrieking at any sound.

Bobby turned to her. "Listen, maybe you'd better walk back down. If the truck starts sliding..."

"What are you going to do?" she asked, watching him crank the engine of the big truck.

"Jasper can't pick up anyone on his phone from here. We're going back to the last switchback so he can get a call through."

From the conversations she had overheard along the way, Laurel knew the paramedics were already at the Walker farm, waiting.

"They can't make it all the way up here with the ambulance,"

Bobby explained. "I'm gonna tell them a shortcut over the phone, then meet them down at Bent Creek. And I may have to winch them out of a few places."

His boot tapped the accelerator, testing the powerful engine.

"Bobby, what can I do to help? There must be something!"

"Ask Jasper. He's running things. Or trying to."

Just then Jasper appeared at the window. His face was a white mask in the moonlight as he yanked open the door beside Laurel, spraying her with rain and cold.

"Bobby," he shouted, "you gotta take it easy backing down the hill and—"

"Jasper," Laurel interrupted, "you're needed here. I can go back and make that call for you. Just tell me what to say."

His eyes flew over Laurel's head to Bobby, then back. "Reckon you could at that." He shoved the cellular phone into her hand. "You go with Bobby; try every few minutes to get through. When you do, give the phone to Bobby."

The next half hour was a nightmare. The truck skidded downhill, lurched, and skidded again until the road leveled off and widened. While Bobby concentrated on handling all the horsepower, Laurel punched telephone numbers into the phone; finally, she got through to Margaret, who was serving coffee to the paramedics and volunteer rescue team, waiting for the call. Laurel scooted closer to Bobby, placing the cellular phone against his right ear. His hands gripped the steering wheel, turning and twisting it along the switchbacks.

"Bo, you drivin' tonight?" he asked. "Okay, listen. You'll have to take that road by the fence on the east side of Mr. Walker's house. It skirts that back meadow, you know. There's a washout there beside the last fence post. Just veer to the right and you'll be

231

okay. Come around Clarence's barn and north up the old logging road. You'll save ten or fifteen minutes that way. And I'll wait for you at the switchback above Bent Creek 'cause your vehicle can't make it all the way."

As Bobby rattled off the route, it occurred to Laurel that no rescue team could have acted more quickly or wisely than the men who had spent their lives in these mountains. *The very people Madeline had dismissed as ignorant.*

"You'd better get out of the truck and wait here," Bobby said as he hung up. "Winching that ambulance out of the low spots can be tricky business. If I wreck, I don't want you along."

Laurel gripped his hand. "Bobby, you can make it. I know you can. Just be very, very careful."

He nodded, and thrust an extra flashlight in her hand. She opened the door and crawled out of the truck, yanking the hood of the slicker over her head. She crept toward the edge of the road to get out of his way, then stood staring after the truck as it roared off down the mountain. Darkness encapsulated her; only the sound of the falling rain broke the silence. To occupy her mind, she thought about the summer and all that had happened. She especially thought about Matt. She loved him; how she loved him! But what was going to happen? Time dragged on.

Laurel had no idea how much time had lapsed when she heard the sound of the truck. She leaped to her feet, straining to hear. The sound grew closer, and soon she could make out the lights of the truck far down the road. Bobby's truck ground its way back up the mountain, accompanied by the ambulance. She moaned with relief as the truck and ambulance moved cautiously along the steep road.

The procession came to a stop several yards from her, and she watched with a grateful heart as three men in white coats baled out, their arms full of equipment.

"Laurel, you'll have to give up your seat," Bobby yelled to her. "I'm taking these guys up the mountain in the truck; then we'll walk down the path to the plane. When we get the people out, we'll load them in the back of the truck and bring them here to the ambulance."

Seventeen

It seemed like an eternity before Laurel heard the truck again. When she did, she ran along the side of the road, unable to wait until the truck reached the parked ambulance.

"Wait," Bobby yelled out the window. "Stay out of the way till we get to the ambulance."

Numbly, Laurel stepped to the side of the road, her heart drumming in her throat. She wanted to leap into the back of the truck to see for herself the Wentworths' condition, but the paramedics were bent over them, and Laurel knew she mustn't distract them. With precision and care, the medics were doing their best to save the lives of Anna Lee, Madeline, and the pilot. Finally the truck backed up to the open doors on the rear of the ambulance.

Laurel crept forward.

Anna Lee's voice was the only one she could hear. She was moaning and sobbing in a strange kind of monotone.

"Anna Lee, I'm here," Laurel called, trying to extend her hand to touch the blanketed body.

The paramedics switched on lights inside the ambulance, grabbing IVs, gurneys, oxygen. They worked swiftly, competently. Through the light streaming from the rear of the ambulance, Laurel had a dim view of the people in the back of the truck. Her hands flew to her mouth, squelching the sobs rising in her throat. She fought for composure, and moved closer, her breath jerking through her chest.

Anna Lee's face had turned blue. The blanket covering her vibrated from spasms going through her body. Her mouth twisted in moans of pain.

"Anna Lee, darling, I'm here," Laurel repeated, as she looked down into the blue eyes, glazed with shock.

At least she's alive, she told herself, trying to take comfort.

The pilot appeared to be in better shape. He was crouched against the cab of the truck, talking in a low voice to one of the paramedics. His clothing was bloodstained, and through the sleeve of his torn shirt, Laurel saw a bone protruding. She winced, looking away.

Then she saw Madeline. Her face was covered with blood, her short hair a mass of red. She was either unconscious or dead; Laurel couldn't be sure either way.

Laurel looked at the man working with Madeline. "Is she going to...?" Her eyes pleaded the question.

He glanced quickly at Laurel's worried face and shook his head.

"Maybe, maybe not," he said.

Laurel stepped back, giving them room. She couldn't reach Anna Lee now, but it wouldn't matter. Anna Lee had passed out.

"Laurel." Robert Walker stood beside her. His clothes were

soaked with rain and mud, and his face held the look of utter exhaustion.

"Come back to the house. You look like you need some hot coffee," he said gently.

Laurel nodded, watching as the ambulance started up and began its descent down the mountain. "I just wish the chopper could have gotten through," she said, staring bleakly at the sky.

"They're in good hands," Robert said, slipping his arm around her. "Once the driver gets farther down, he'll open up the siren and they'll have them at the hospital in no time."

"I want to go with them," she said, tears trickling down her cheeks.

"Jasper can take you to the hospital, but first I insist on you coming back to the house and warming up a bit."

She nodded, knowing what he said made sense. She glanced over her shoulder and saw the men grouped together, talking in low voices. From the expressions on their faces, they believed Anna Lee was dying and Madeline was already gone.

She couldn't bring herself to ask any questions, not now. She still believed in miracles.

It was twelve minutes after ten when Laurel pulled into the hospital parking lot and locked her car. While the horrible night seemed to go on forever, she was surprised to learn the plane had gone down only two hours before.

Her eyes scanned the parking lot, automatically looking for Matt's black Jeep before she remembered he was flying back. Flying back! She wondered, after looking at Anna Lee and Madeline, if she could ever get on another plane, large or small.

She rushed through the electronic doors of the emergency unit, then stopped, bewildered. Across the waiting area, she met a sea of weary faces. Spotting the reception desk, she hurried forward.

"Excuse me, I'm with the Wentworth family."

"Are you part of the family?" the receptionist asked, shuffling through papers.

"No, I'm a friend."

"Just a minute, please."

Laurel nodded, turning to scan the room again. As she did, she heard the glass front doors slide open to admit a man in a gray windbreaker.

Her heart lurched.

"Matt," she cried, rushing to his side.

His eyes were bleak as he reached for her. His windbreaker smelled of the rain mixed with his spicy cologne, and she could feel his heart beating through the jacket as she hugged him.

"Laurel! Where...how...?"

"I just got here," she said, looking up into his face, trying not to cry. Instinctively her arms wound around his neck, and she kissed him briefly. She felt so sorry for him and his family.

"Thanks for being here," he said, gripping her hand as they hurried to the desk.

"I'm Matt Wentworth," he announced to the receptionist.

The woman stood. "Come this way." She glanced at Laurel. "You can come, too."

They followed the nurse through a set of double doors, down a long hall, and around a corner to a small, private room holding a leather loveseat and a couple of chairs.

"I'll get a doctor to come and speak to you," she said.

Laurel swallowed, unsure just what this meant. If they weren't being taken back to the treatment room, had Anna Lee and Mrs. Wentworth...? She couldn't bear to think the word.

The door opened and a man dressed in green with a surgical mask around his neck stepped inside. He extended his hand. "Hello, I'm Dr. Cohn."

Matt stood, extending his hand. "I'm Matt Wentworth, and this is my friend Laurel Hollingsworth. How are my mother and sister?"

The doctor looked worried. "Your sister is in shock, but she's going to be all right. Her right ankle is broken, and she has some minor cuts and bruises—nothing that won't heal."

"Thank God." Matt breathed a sigh. "And Mother?"

The doctor glanced from Matt to Laurel and back.

"Dr. Joseph, our neurosurgeon is seeing her now. He'll be coming to talk with you soon. She sustained an injury to her head, and has multiple broken ribs. There are some other cuts and bruises, but our main concern, of course, is her head." He paused, studying Matt's face for his reaction thus far.

"She's critical," Matt finished for him.

"Very critical," the doctor replied. "We're doing all we can for both of them."

"How's Jack Freeman? He was flying the plane," Matt explained.

"He has a broken arm and leg, but otherwise, he'll be fine."

Matt nodded. "From what I understand, he performed a miraculous feat, getting that plane down." He took a deep breath.

Dr. Cohn nodded. "Dr. Jos ph will be in shortly."

As he walked out, Laurel put her arms around Matt, hugging him gently. "I'll be right here with you, for as long as you need me."

Matt's eyes were fatigued, worried, yet hopeful as he gazed into Laurel's face, hugging her back. He ran his finger along her cheek and looked deeply into her eyes. "I'll always need you," he said quietly.

Eighteen

aurel decided to take Matt's advice and try to get some rest. She had been driving back and forth from Angel Valley to Knoxville for the past week. During the first crucial night and day, she had slept in the ICU waiting room until Anna Lee was moved to a private room and the doctors assured Matt that she was out of danger.

The pilot had explained everything to Matt. A problem had developed soon after takeoff. He had been forced to land as best he could. Amazingly, he had lowered the plane slowly, finding enough level land while narrowly escaping the side of the mountain. Despite his skill, the emergency landing could have killed them all. Yet only Madeline remained critical.

Laurel walked down the hall to the waiting room for ICU. Tenderness filled her eyes as she looked at Matt, dozing in a chair. She felt a strong urge to go over and kiss his whiskered cheek, but she did not want to wake him. He'd had very little sleep. During scheduled times, families were allowed behind the big doors of intensive care to see their loved ones who hung between life and death. With his father gone, Matt felt the responsibility of being there for Madeline, in case she came out of her coma.

People stirred around her, and she noticed visiting hours had just opened. She glanced at Matt, wishing he could rest. His mother wouldn't know if he were at her side, anyway. She hesitated, watching the people slip quietly through the metal doors to visit their loved ones. Placing her shoulder bag in a chair beside Matt—who still slept—she turned and followed. A nurse or doctor might have some new information on Madeline's condition.

She knew where to find Madeline, for she had already been in with Matt that first night, hoping to comfort him. She stepped quickly into the room where a nurse leaned over the bed, checking the IV in Madeline's arm.

There was an oxygen tube in her nose, an IV in her arm, and monitors and machines surrounded the bed. Madeline was oblivious to everything. Her face seemed whiter than the sheet and the bandage on her head. It was an absolute miracle that she had survived those first hours after losing so much blood when she was already in frail health.

She had been taken to surgery as soon as Matt arrived to give consent. Afterward, the neurosurgeons had been honest: her chances for survival were slim.

The nurse checked the monitors, writing something on a chart as Laurel approached the bed where Madeline laid, still as death. The woman who had once been so forceful and domineering, looked frail and helpless.

Laurel drew a deep breath as a feeling of pity swept over her. Madeline was lucky to be alive. No, it wasn't luck that had saved her, although she imagined Madeline would call it that.

"Any change?" Laurel looked at the nurse.

"She's a little better," she smiled. "I'll be right back."

Laurel nodded as her eyes moved slowly over the medical equipment surrounding the bed. She took a step closer. Madeline's left arm was unbandaged, her fingers curled against the white sheets.

Gently, Laurel touched her arm. The skin was cold beneath Laurel's fingers. This woman had given birth to the man Laurel loved, to the man who was kind and sensitive and caring and wanted to help other people. Deep within Madeline's soul, there had to be goodness as well. She just had not been strong enough to deal with the disappointments, the struggles, the loss of her husband.

Without realizing what she was doing, Laurel gently stroked Madeline's arm as she looked into the woman's thin face, wondering about her. Then she closed her eyes and prayed.

"God, give her the strength to survive this, please. Touch her and heal her; make her well again."

When Laurel opened her eyes, Madeline stared at her.

Laurel gasped. The blue eyes that had looked at Laurel so coldly in the past were now fixed on her with an expression that was completely blank. Laurel froze, wondering what to say, what to do. Madeline said nothing, showed no signs of recognition before closing her eyes again. Laurel released her pent-up breath. It hadn't registered with Madeline that the person she hated so much stood by her bed, praying for her.

Soft footsteps whispered over the floor, and Laurel glanced back to see the nurse returning to the bed.

"She woke up," Laurel burst out, then bit her lip, glancing around, remembering she was supposed to be quiet. "She opened her eyes and looked at me."

The nurse rushed to the bed, murmuring softly to Madeline, trying to wake her again. Laurel rushed back to the waiting room to get Matt. Perhaps Madeline would respond to him; perhaps there was hope.

Nineteen

Laurel sat beside the hospital bed, clutching Anna Lee's hand. "You're going to be fine," she said, smiling down into Anna Lee's swollen face.

"God took care of us," Anna Lee said. "I just kept reading those verses you gave me. I had them in my purse and I read them aloud, over and over. I know he saved us, Laurel; I know he did."

"I know he did, too," Matt said, from behind Laurel.

She turned in her seat to look over her shoulder at him. It was amazing to realize that during the long and horrible ordeal some good things had happened.

"Laurel," Matt placed a gentle hand on her shoulder, "Mother would like to speak with you. Would you mind going to ICU? I'll sit here and have a chat with Sis."

Laurel nodded, her eyes lingering on Matt. He looked fresh and rested; his blue eyes were bright with hope.

Hesitantly, Laurel got out of her chair and walked to the intensive care unit. While it was only a short walk, every step grew heavier and heavier as Laurel thought about facing Madeline. Why did she want to see her? Was she going to tell her to stay away from Matt and Anna Lee?

Laurel squared her shoulders and entered the room. The nurse was standing beside the bed, smoothing out the covers.

"You're doing better," she said, smiling at her patient. "Oh, hello," she glanced across at Laurel.

Laurel smiled. "Hello."

Laurel's eyes drifted to the bed and she hesitated, wondering what to say to Madeline as her thin face rolled on the pillow and her pale eyes found Laurel.

She motioned Laurel to come closer, and Laurel stepped quickly to the bed.

Dark circles ringed Madeline's pale blue eyes, which seemed to have sunken deeply in their sockets. She had lost several pounds and looked absolutely gaunt. Laurel wondered if she was going to make it, even though the doctors were now hopeful.

"How are you feeling?" Laurel asked, smiling down at her.

"Better," Madeline rasped. "Thank you for your prayers." She spoke each word slowly, as though talking was an extremely tiring task.

"You're welcome. Everyone in Angel Valley is praying." The words rolled from Laurel's lips in a burst of enthusiasm, then she clamped her mouth shut. Maybe Madeline wouldn't want to hear that.

"I had no idea people could be so kind. Matt has told me what the people did to rescue us." She hesitated, taking a deep breath. "I've been so unfair. To everyone in Angel Valley. Especially to you. You've helped Anna Lee more than anyone, and you've made Matt happy."

Laurel caught her breath, unable to speak, although she didn't think a response was expected. She could see that Madeline wanted to talk, but Laurel wondered if she should be exerting so much energy.

Madeline looked at Laurel in a different way, and Laurel saw tears forming in the eyes that had been so hard in the past weeks. "When I saw you standing here, praying for me," she continued haltingly, "I wondered how you could be so forgiving."

"Mrs. Wentworth, I care about you. And you've already apologized, so please don't tire yourself."

"You've shown me the meaning of Christianity," Madeline continued in a shaky voice, as the tears overflowed onto her wrinkled cheeks. "I grew up in poverty. We had nothing. My parents had a different kind of religion...hard...and punishing. When I left home, I wanted to leave all the hard things behind."

She took a deep breath then flinched. She closed her eyes for a moment as though waiting for the pain to subside. Then slowly her eyes opened again, and as she looked at Laurel, a tiny smile formed on her wrinkled lips. "You and your people have shown me a different kind of faith. Thank you, Laurel," she said, reaching for her hand.

Laurel grasped Madeline's cold fingers, squeezing gently. When the woman tried to grip her hand, Laurel realized she had no strength left.

"You're welcome, Mrs. Wentworth."

The nurse returned to the room, and as her eyes swept over her patient, she checked her pulse. "She needs to rest," she said, looking at Laurel.

"Okay, I'll go now." Laurel glanced back at Madeline, who was already asleep. She could hardly believe her words, and certainly never expected it. She swallowed hard, amazed by the change. Stopping at the nurses' station, she waited until one had a free moment to speak with her. Finally, one looked up and smiled.

"Excuse me, is Mrs. Wentworth going to be all right?" Laurel asked.

The nurse nodded. "We think so. The doctor has given permission for Mrs. Wentworth and Anna Lee to be flown back to Atlanta in another week if they continue to make progress." She leaned back in the chair, her eyes filled with wonder. "It's a miracle."

Laurel nodded. "Yes, I know."

The prayers, the efforts of Angel Valley's people, and the skill of doctors and medicine had combined to save their lives. And the final miracle was that Madeline had found God again.

As Laurel stepped back into the hall, she came upon Matt, waiting by the door. She turned her eyes up to him, her face filled with wonder.

"She was very kind. I'm so glad she's going to be all right."

Matt nodded as he put his arm around her shoulder and they began to walk. "Mother was taking too much medicine for her migraines. In fact, she was headed for a breakdown. She's been spared." He looked at Laurel. "You were right. This valley is guarded by angels." He smiled into her eyes. "Let's go down to the cafeteria and get some coffee." He hugged her against him. "I have a few things to say to you, too."

After they had ordered sandwiches and drinks and taken a seat in the cafeteria, Matt looked at Laurel for a long time without speaking.

"What is it?" she asked. She knew he had been worried sick over his mother and sister during the past two weeks. Today, for the first time, he seemed to relax.

"How can I ever thank you?" he asked.

"You already have, at least a hundred times."

She put down her fork and reached over to squeeze his hand.

"I should be thanking you, as well."

He lifted an eyebrow. "For what?"

"For being the kind of man you are. For all you've done for the people in Angel Valley. And for Granny's carpet." Her eyes twinkled as she waited for a response.

This time he didn't bother denying it, although Laurel suspected he might not admit it, either. She tried a different approach.

"The problem is, Granny may want to swap some of it in on a different color for the back bedroom. Just give me the salesman's name, and I won't have to bother you about it again."

He had just bit into his hamburger, so it was several seconds before he looked at her with a mischievous grin.

"You'll have to talk to Melissa, my assistant in Atlanta. She handled it for me."

"I knew it," Laurel whooped, startling those dining at the adjoining table. "It was you, after all." She nodded her head, satisfied. "It was you."

An expression of surprise flitted over his face for a moment, then he chuckled. "You tricked me."

"Well, she might want to change the carpet. Then again," she began to laugh, "she might not. But Matt, you shouldn't have."

"I should have! It's the least I can do for her. After all, she's your grandmother, and she's quickly becoming one of my closest friends."

Laurel smiled at him, then returned to her sandwich. There was no point in trying to give him back the money; he wouldn't take it.

"Since you're determined to have a little debate going as we eat, here's another one." He took a sip of his soda, then looked across at her. "How would you feel about my living in Angel Valley full time?"

"Do you mean it?" she asked, staring at him, unable to believe what he had just asked her.

"No, I'm just teasing." He reached over, playfully tapping the tip of her nose. "Of course I mean it, silly."

"But..."

"I'm going to open an office in Knoxville. Mr. Benson, the man who was Dad's right arm all these years, can take over the Atlanta office. I think it's time the company branched out a bit. Knoxville would be a good place to start, and it's a comfortable commuting distance from Angel Valley. And now, I can oversee the project we've started here."

As she listened, her heart soared with joy. Their jobs and lifestyles had seemed like an insurmountable hurdle to their relationship. Suddenly one miracle after another was unfolding before her, and she could hardly take it all in.

"So what do you think of having me around all the time?"

"You know I would be thrilled beyond words." She leaned over to kiss his cheek.

He reached for her hand, and for a moment neither spoke. They just sat there, gazing into one another's eyes.

The waitress smiled at the couple who were obviously very much in love. "Excuse me," she cleared her throat, "we need to close the dining area in the next fifteen minutes. We'll reopen at five."

They came out of their reverie and hurried through their meal. As they left the cafeteria, Laurel slipped her hand in Matt's and pressed her head against his shoulder. The storm of terror and worry had passed. They had survived the long dark night to discover a new day of joy. There would be other problems, of course, but suddenly with Matt beside her and a strong love growing in her heart, Laurel felt certain they could make it through.

$\mathcal{T}wenty$

Snowflakes feathered down over the merry crowd clustered together in the park. It was a frosty night, with the temperature dropping to the thirties, but there was no wind, and everyone was bundled in heavy coats with scarves and caps, thick gloves, and warm boots. No one seemed to mind the cold, for all eyes held that magical glow of Christmas, as voices lifted in a spirited rendition of "Oh, Holy Night." Hundreds of candles flickered in a sea of golden light as the words rang out loud and clear. "A thrill of hope, the weary world rejoices, for yonder breaks a new and glorious morn..."

The crowd huddled together, everyone singing, even Laurel, not caring about her off-key notes in the joy of the moment.

She stood beside Matt, her gloved hand thrust into the warm pocket of his overcoat, as they raised their voices in song. Occasionally they turned to face one another, smiling, as the voices around them swelled to a crescendo, then softly died away with the ending of the song.

Afterward, the pastor stepped forward, inviting everyone to

adjourn to the community center where refreshments would be served.

Everyone began to talk at once, their breath creating tiny clouds around their faces.

"Coming, Granny?" Matt glanced back at the little woman, bundled to the chin, yet sporting a bright red nose.

"Right behind you," she called through chattering teeth.

Laurel squeezed Matt's arm. "I wish your mother and Anna Lee could have come."

Matt nodded. "Anna Lee's so involved with her school drama group she never wants to miss a meeting, and Mother isn't up to being out in the cold. She'll come up next spring." He smiled down at Laurel.

The group headed toward the corner of the block where Fats's service station had once huddled. His property had been purchased for a more noble cause, and he was now the proud owner of a new service station on the edge of town, more suitable for his business. The old building had been leveled, the dirty concrete chipped up, hauled off, and the land smoothed out. A new log building graced the corner, built by men of Angel Valley who needed work. While the building maintained the rustic look of the town, there was a wonderful fresh cedar smell upon entering the huge front room, where tables were spread with food. At the far end, an enormous stone fireplace offered a blazing fire to those needing warmth, while local carvings and handiwork surrounded the hearth.

Throughout the room, symbols of local talent were displayed: paintings, woodwork, quilts, candles and pottery, even a finely-carved cupboard where bell jars of blackberry jam, apple butter, and sourwood honey were displayed. Harold's rockers graced the room, while the adjoining building housed the working tools and storage space for the artists. A pot-bellied stove and a fully equipped kitchen had turned the room into a gathering place. The only disadvantage was that the social life sometimes played havoc with the artists at work. Nobody was working on this Christmas Eve, however. Nor would the new trucks, parked behind the building, be rolling out of town until after the New Year, carrying items to be sold all over the country.

It was a time of rejoicing, of giving thanks to family, friends, and most of all to God for all the blessings of life.

Millie busily directed young people with serving trays of gingerbread men, peanut brittle, and cookies and cake from the huge kitchen in the rear. Other women bustled about, seeing to the long tables of food where urns of hot cider waited.

Billy, dressed in a Santa Claus suit minus the cap, laughed and played chase with the children until Robert Walker quieted the group down, announcing it was time to say grace. Robert lifted his hands to the group, motioning for silence.

"Before the pastor says grace," Robert began, waving his hands once more to silence the group, "we have a little ceremony to attend to here."

Clarence stepped forward, handing Robert a small plaque, with a name and inscription exquisitely carved into it.

Robert glanced over the plaque, nodding approval, before gazing out over the silent crowd.

"The folks of Angel Valley would like to express our appreciation to Matthew Wentworth and his family for the contribution they've made here." He paused, allowing his eyes to wander over the remarkable building. "We owe you a debt of gratitude, Matt," he finished among rowdy cheers.

Matt glanced down into Laurel's face. Her eyes were sparkling with tears as he squeezed her hand and left her. On his way to the podium, he looked around him, smiling, speaking to friends. When he reached Robert's side, a hush fell over the crowd.

"Thank you," he said, accepting the plaque and reading its inscription. "I'll treasure this always." He looked back at the people whose eyes were shining with admiration as they listened to him speak. "I'll put it over the desk in my new office next door."

He hesitated, as his eyes moved back over the crowd, pausing on Laurel. "I feel that I'm the one who owes the debt of gratitude to you people for allowing me to be a part of your lives. I was told back in the summer that this was the most wonderful place on earth," he smiled tenderly, "by the most wonderful woman on earth. Thanks to you people and your talent, our little business is thriving. We'll never get rich," his smile widened, "but that's not the object. We're sending your special work all over the country, and you've helped fulfill my own personal dream of being able to live here and marry the woman I love so very much."

Cheers shook the rafters.

"You're all invited to the wedding on New Year's Day." He motioned Laurel to his side. "We thought we'd start the new year off right."

Another round of applause thundered through the hall.

Laurel had made her way through the happy group to his side, slipped her hand in his, and smiled at the people she loved. Tears of joy rolled down her cheeks, and although she impatiently tried to stop them, it was useless.

A few other sniffs could be heard across the room as Laurel

gave up and laughed through her tears before she turned to look at Matt, her face wreathed in the glow of love.

"Happy New Year," she said, happy tears streaming down her face.

"And hundreds more," he chuckled, kissing her while everyone hugged and laughed and cried along with them, and Billy burst into a lively rendition of "Jingle Bells."

Dear Reader:

Angel Valley is a fictitious community set in the Smoky Mountains of Tennessee; however, it could be one of many communities that still exist in this unique state. I am proud to be a native Tennessean, and I wanted to create a setting that was a composite of these communities "where everyone knows your name" and where neighbors really care about one another. Maybe it will provoke a pleasant memory for some of you, or provide a little escape for others who live in cities and long for that "small town atmosphere." As for the characters in Angel Valley, they, too, are composites of small town life or, in the case of the Wentworths, people who can benefit from good, old fashioned values.

I first toured the Smokies with my college sweetheart while a student at the University of Tennessee in nearby Knoxville. since then, the college sweetheart has become my husband and we have returned many times with our family. We have lived in some beautiful areas—Canada, Colorado, Alabama—but in my mind no place can match the beauty of the Smokies and the neighboring Blue Ridge Parkway.

As I finish this novel, I realize with a bit of a shock that this is my tenth one. Writing is a labor of love for me, and I am grateful to all the readers for their continued support. I pray that you will enjoy the setting and the characters of Angel Valley as much as I have.

Love and blessings to all of you,

Peggy Darty

Peggy Darty
c/o Palisades
P.O. Box 1720
Sisters, Oregon 97759

Palisades...Pure Romance

Refuge, Lisa Tawn Bergren
Torchlight, Lisa Tawn Bergren
Treasure, Lisa Tawn Bergren
Secrets, Robin Jones Gunn
Sierra, Shari MacDonald
Westward, Amanda MacLean
Glory, Marilyn Kok
Love Song, Sharon Gillenwater
Cherish, Constance Colson
Whispers, Robin Jones Gunn
Angel Valley, Peggy Darty
Stonehaven, Amanda MacLean (August)
Antiques, Sharon Gillenwater (September)
A Christmas Joy, Darty, Gillenwater, MacLean (October)

Titles and dates are subject to change.